*To Jane —
Enjoy!
Bonnie J. Cardone*

THE Fireside Diver

An Anthology of

Underwater Adventure

Collected and edited

by Bonnie J. Cardone

AQUA QUEST PUBLICATIONS, INC.
—NEW YORK—

FREE CATALOG
Aqua Quest Publications, Inc. publishes and
distributes books on underwater photography, wreck
diving, marine life, travel destinations, technical
diving and safety. If these books are not available at
your local book or dive store, write or call us directly
for a catalog of our publications.

AQUA QUEST PUBLICATIONS, INC.
Post Office Box 700
Locust Valley, NY 11560-0700

1-800-933-8989   516-759-0476

Library of Congress Cataloging-in-Publication Data

The fireside diver : an anthology of underwater adventure by
  more than 20 of the best writers on & under the sea /
  edited by Bonnie Cardone.
      p.   cm.
  Originally published : Birmingham, Ala. : Menasha
Ridge Press, 1992.
  Includes bibliographical references (p.   ).
  ISBN 1-881652-09-2 : $14.95 (pbk.)
  1. Scuba diving. I. Cardone, Bonnie J., 1942-
GV840.S78F576 1995
797.2'3–dc20   95-32810
                                                        CIP

Text design by April Leidig-Higgins
Cover design by Paul Bacon

Printed in the United States of America
10 9 8 7 6 5 4 3 2

To divers:

the most adventurous

people I know

CONTENTS

ix

FOREWORD

I n 1973 I was a full-time housewife and mother of two young children. Since moving to Southern California six years earlier I had often seen groups of black-clad divers gathered on the Pacific Ocean beaches in the early hours of weekend mornings. I loved the water, was an excellent swimmer, and had often thought of taking scuba lessons. Another class I had signed up for had been cancelled that spring and, not long after, the mail brought a flier from the Palisades YMCA. I signed up for the scuba class offered immediately, although not without some trepidation, since I was sure the Pacific was shark infested.

The class was three weeks long. There were three-hour lectures on Tuesday nights, three hours of poolwork on Thursday nights, and several hours of open water work on each of three weekend mornings. It was incredibly exciting and challenging, both physically and mentally. Once we got to the part about physiology and I learned about the bends, nitrogen narcosis, and embolisms, I stopped worrying about sharks—there were too many other things to think about!

My class started out with about eight people, but by the time we were ready to graduate there were only three of us left. I passed my written exam and on Sunday, June 9, 1973, made my first two dives off Catalina Island. The water was cold, but clear. I thought the underwater scene was beautiful, especially so after the sand-laden waters of our class beach dives.

Those several weeks in 1973 changed my life. In the years since then I have dived with hammerhead sharks and manta rays in the Sea of Cortez; experienced the exhilarating deep walls of the Cayman Islands; photographed the friendly marine life of Bonaire; visited deep shipwrecks off North Carolina; learned to identify seashells off Hawaii; and been shipwrecked in the South China Sea. Still, most of my diving has been off the California coast. From Santa Barbara to San Diego, I have dived with sea lions and blue sharks (on purpose!), visited shipwrecks both deep and shallow, become familiar with the waters surrounding all eight channel islands as well as several of their offshore pinnacles; and worked at the challenging job of photographing what I find in this underwater wonderland.

My own adventures pale when compared to others you will find in this book. Although I did not intend to concentrate on stories by underwater photographers, it seems they are the ones not only leading adventurous lives but writing the articles and taking the pictures that document those adventures.

Diving has changed my life, sending me in directions and to places I never dreamed I'd go. I would venture a guess that everyone whose work can be found in this book would say the same. Come share our adventures.

Bonnie J. Cardone

ACKNOWLEDGMENTS

I became acquainted with most of the authors whose work appears in this book through *Skin Diver Magazine*, whose pages I have edited since 1976. These people are an interesting lot—all of them exploring and expanding the frontiers of diving—and I am proud to call many of them friends. To a man (and/or woman), they were models of cooperation and helpfulness. Thank you, everyone!

Thanks also to Bob Sehlinger, who suggested this project and provided encouragement and advice.

A special thanks to Paul Tzimoulis and Bill Gleason of *Skin Diver*, who continue to employ me in a position that allows me to meet and work with the world's top underwater photographers and writers.

HOWARD HALL

A wildlife film producer who specializes in marine subjects, Howard Hall has won four Emmys for his cinematography. His film for the PBS series "Nature," *Seasons in the Sea,* won the prestigious Wildscreen award in 1990. A second "Nature" film, *Shadows in a Desert Sea,* premiered in 1992. Howard is currently at work on a special for National Geographic Television, scheduled to air in 1994.

Howard has also written and illustrated several books including, *Successful Underwater Photography, Sharks: The Perfect Predator, The Kelp Forest,* and *A Charm of Dolphins.* Not one to take himself or nearly anything else (except filmmaking) seriously for very long, Howard says his other accomplishments include being "a good hang glider pilot, a poor snow skier, and an even poorer surfer. My biggest claim to fame" he adds," is that I can hold my breath longer than any surviving member of my third grade class."

HOWARD HALL

Hammerheads
by the Hundreds

As I lay on the surface hyperventilating, I stared at a point directly below where shimmering rays of sunlight converged on my shadow. I was trying desperately to relax; to slow my heart rate to normal or, hopefully, even slower. Years of experience had taught me how much hyperventilation I could tolerate before passing out during my ascent. This dive, however, was important and I had no idea how many others I would have. I intended to press the limits a bit. The 16mm movie camera in my hand weighed 40 pounds above water and though it is nearly neutral in the water, I had to remember it would create considerable drag and account for that in my timing. Fifty feet below, the shadows were moving in my direction.

I took an extremely deep breath of air and then gulped several additional mouthfuls into my lungs, filling them to absolute capacity. Then as slowly and as efficiently as possible, I bent at the waist, raised my legs and dived. During the first 40 feet of descent, I closed my eyes and listened to the sound of my heart as the pulse became slower and slower. Then after reaching a point where my buoyancy had become negative, I allowed myself to sink. Finally, at 70 feet I leveled out and slowly began swimming toward the approaching shadows. To get the best possible camera angle, I had to get below the school. As I looked up, I realized that, indeed, the school was going to pass right above me. I pointed the camera skyward and pulled the trigger.

It was like looking at a school of bait passing overhead. There were literally hundreds of them, but these were not tiny fish, these creatures were seven to ten feet in length. Even one of these massive animals normally produces terror in the hearts of inexperienced divers and, yet, directly above me were clouds of them. Clouds of hammerhead sharks!

I continued to film until the enormous school of sharks was directly above, but by then my breath was gone. The scene above was exactly what I had dreamed of filming for the last several months, but I had to ascend immediately or risk staying there indefinitely. I dropped the camera to my waist and began ascending directly into the school of approximately 400 hammerhead sharks that swam above me. Suddenly, I was inside the school. I wished I could stop and film. The sharks were everywhere and very close; closer than I had hoped to get. But I couldn't stop. At this point, the effort necessary to raise the camera and film would be too costly.

As I turned, I saw that one shark was on a collision course with me! I hesitated for a moment and it passed over my head with only inches to spare. I hit the surface and took one breath and held it while the dizziness passed. The hammerheads were still below, but moving slowly away. I realized they would be gone before I could catch my breath and dive again. It might be hours or even days before I got another chance. But, fortunately, this dive had been productive.

Now, some of you reading this may think anyone purposely placing himself in a school of 400 hammerhead sharks must be

In between Baja California and the Mexican mainland lies a body of water known as the Sea of Cortez. Divers have been encoutering schools of hammerhead sharks here for more than 30 years. Photo by Howard Hall.

quite insane. Certainly hammerheads can be some of the most dangerous sharks in the ocean. But sharks, like all creatures on this planet, demonstrate a variety of behaviors and although they have been described as merely eating machines (that occasionally and indiscriminately eat people), recent studies by a variety of scientists have found them to be far more than that. Each species of shark has its own characteristic behaviors that vary with time of year, time of day, availability of food, and perhaps simply the shark's mood. In 1979 I became aware of studies being made on the schooling behavior of hammerhead sharks in the Sea of Cortez by Dr. Don Nelson, Peter Klimley, and Jeremiah Sullivan. I had seen some tantalizing film footage shot by Dr. Ted Rulison showing these schools of sharks and I was intrigued.

With the help of Stuart Goodman in New York and the staff of ABC sports, I assembled a film crew. In August of 1980, we set out to film these incredible animals.

The film crew assembled by Goodman and myself included some of the most impressive talents in the dive community. The principals in the film were to be author, Peter Benchley; underwater filmmaker, Stan Waterman; and the man who shot that first incredible footage of the schools, Dr. Ted Rulison. In addition to their responsibilities as on-camera talents, Stan and Ted would also help shoot underwater film when possible. The bulk of the underwater filming fell to myself and Gordy Waterman. Although Gordy certainly got his start assisting his famous father, he is now a completely capable and very talented underwater cameraman in his own right. Footage produced by Gordy always seemed to complement my own and vice versa. And on those occasions both Gordy and I missed the best possible shot, Stan always seemed to get it despite his own on camera priorities.

To film the hammerheads, we chartered Baja Expeditions' *Don Jose*. It was perfectly suited for our task. In August we traveled from La Paz to a tiny seamount north of San Jose Island. There we were to spend our next ten days searching for schooling hammerhead sharks.

We anchored the boat at 10:00AM. I got in the water with a mask immediately, followed by my assistant, Marty Snyderman. My excuse was that I wanted to check conditions and inspect the top of the pinnacle, but actually I was hoping to see a hammerhead or two right off. Producing a film like this is an expensive proposition and since success or failure depends entirely on the presence of the sharks, seeing one or two right off would greatly settle the nerves of both myself and Stuart Goodman. I reached the anchorline and looked down through the clear water to the peak 60 feet below. Immediately, I saw six hammerheads pass over the seamount and disappear into the deep water on the far side. I signaled Marty to return to the boat; we had been in the water five minutes.

The concept of the film was to photograph Stan, Peter, and Ted diving among the schooling hammerheads. After the dives Dyanna Taylor and Dave Conley filmed the three as they discussed their experiences and speculated on the reasons for the sharks' behavior. These discussions were recorded on tape by our sound man, Steve Gagne. But, the Sea of Cortez seamount proved so dramatic that the schools of sharks were only shown several times in the film. In addition to swimming amid hundreds of hammerhead sharks, we also filmed sailfish, marlin, sea lions, tuna, and an amazing encounter with a giant manta ray that encouraged us to ride upon its back! We had brought far more film than we thought we could use, but we returned without an unexposed frame.

As I look back on the expedition now, however, the single most impressive sight is still that silhouette of literally hundreds of hammerhead sharks hanging above me as I held my breath at 70 feet. The idea of such an experience would have scared me to death at one time in my dive career. But I have learned much about sharks in recent years. I now know that many of the classical concepts of this wonderful creature are invalid. Certainly sharks can be dangerous, but not all species of sharks. And those that must be considered potentially dangerous may not be dangerous at all times. The reasons these animals occasionally bite humans may be far more complicated than we suspect.

The case of the schooling hammerheads is especially interesting. During this type of behavior, the sharks seem totally non-aggressive to, or even shy of, divers and they don't seem to be

Hammerheads are predictably found on El Bajo seamount. They seem leary of the sound of scuba; the best photographs of them are taken by free divers. Photo by Howard Hall.

attracted to baits.   Dr. Nelson, Peter Klimley and Jeremiah Sullivan have been studying this behavior for several years. Although they suspect schooling may be related to mating, they have found very little proof. As yet, the answer is far from clear. Normally, sharks don't school.

This species of shark (the scalloped hammerhead) can be dangerous during other moods, however. Several years ago while we were filming blue sharks off the coast of San Diego, a scalloped hammerhead came in and attacked cameraman Larry Cochrane. He survived by inserting his movie camera into the shark's mouth each time it tried to bite him. Since the camera was running at the time, the incident produced a rather dramatic piece of footage. Although this shark came in eagerly to bait, the sharks in the Sea of Cortez were not interested by baits we placed on the top of the seamount even when they swam right over them.

The ten days I spent in the Sea of Cortez during this film expedition were perhaps the most memorable days of my dive career. Each of us made dozens of dives and on each dive we saw hammerheads; often dozens of them. In fact, it is really something to dive in an area, watching manta rays, billfish and schools of hammerhead sharks passing by. It is experiences like this that make scuba diving the most wonderful way of life on earth.

Fantasy Flight

anging on the anchorline of the *Don Jose* while waiting for an experience that would carry me off into fantasy, I was feeling slightly guilty for leaving my movie camera and filming responsibilities above. But I could not allow this opportunity to pass me by. I had faithfully filmed the phenomenon as everybody else on the film team rode. Now at last, alone, tired, all but dived out, my decompression meter too close to the red zone, I was determined to have my turn.

As I scanned the dark water on the far side of the seamount for the winged creature, I wondered if the others appreciated the significance of what was happening here. Surely if the writers of fantasy had this chance they would appreciate it. They have written of it in countless stories of imaginary worlds. The Hobbits are rescued from the Dark Mountain by the King of the Eagles and fly away astride the shoulders of the great bird. And, in a world called Pern, the heroes fly through the clouds on the backs of winged dragons. They are the *Dragon Riders of Pern*. What child hasn't dreamed of flying off into wind-swept skies on the back of his own winged beast?

But, as children grow into adults, these dreams fade. Oh, we may still be entertained occasionally by the skilled writings of

A fantasy come true: A diver rides a huge manta ray in Mexico's Sea of Cortez. Photo by Howard Hall.

dreamers, but we haven't the time to waste on wishing for things impossible. Yet childhood dreams never fade away entirely, and impossible is not always an absolute.

A movement on the edge of visibility snapped me out of my daydream like the crack of a whip. My heart began to pound as a dark shape materialized into a great winged beast flying toward me. Once again I was awed by his size. From wing tip to wing tip he measured, at the very least, 18 and probably closer to 20 feet. His eyes were a full three feet apart! He was ten feet long from his head to the base of his tail! We had named him Grandad and he was the largest manta ray we had ever seen.

Grandad approached until he was directly below me, then,

predictably, he seemed to deliberately hesitate as I released the anchorline and drifted down toward him. As I descended, my view of the bottom was completely blocked by the huge ray. It was like landing on the seamount itself. Gently I grasped the shoulders of Grandad's wings and felt the surge of power go through his body as his massive wings began to beat. The water began rushing past my face, sucking my exhaust bubbles down across my back and along my legs. Then, holding fast to Grandad's enormous shoulders, I flew off into the dark, deep waters beyond the edge of the seamount. Reality had become fantasy, and fantasy had become real.

It is not clear why this manta allowed our film crew to ride upon its back. Certainly, its slightest shrug would send its fragile rider tumbling. In fact, the manta did shrug once, leaving Stan Waterman with a bloodied lip. And, once the ray did an outside loop that was too much for Peter Benchley and sent him tumbling. Stan, Peter, and Dr. Ted Rulison were the stars of our film and all three rode Grandad at once on several occasions, with room for more.

When Grandad first showed up at the seamount we noticed that a large heavy rope was tangled around his head. Gordy Waterman and Dyanna Taylor followed the manta for an entire dive in efforts to cut the line off. The rope had been there a long time and was deeply embedded in the ray's flesh. Toward the end of the dive Gordy finally succeeded in removing most of the line. Later that day Grandad allowed Michele Binder to ride on his back and remove the remainder of the rope. Since the divers had rid the manta of a painful "thorn," some crew members thought that perhaps the animal regarded us as large cleaner fish. It did seem as if the manta actually encouraged us to ride upon its back.

Grandad carried me out into the open water beyond the

seamount and then he began to descend. At 100 feet he leveled off and went into a steep right bank raising his left wing high toward the sunlit surface and dropping his right wing toward the dark water below. As Grandad turned, I was able to look straight down and saw the bottom about 40 feet below. I had expected the water to be much deeper here and I knew we were well away from the seamount. Then I saw a dark cliff rise before us. It was a second pinnacle—an area we had searched for and had spent days finding. Grandad had found it moments after the beginning of our ride.

Once again Grandad banked right and I knew he was heading back in the general direction of the seamount. He continued to descend following the bottom contour between the pinnacles. Looking over Grandad's shoulders I saw hundreds of magnificent gorgonians in dozens of colors as the bottom rushed past. We dipped beneath a beautifully delicate jellyfish and in the distance I saw a small group of hammerhead sharks pass by. I was living a dream and yet I knew I must check my decompression meter: the sight of the needle in the red zone would bring back an unwelcome reality. But, Grandad insisted upon descending.

My ride ended at a depth of 120 feet. I simply couldn't stay down any longer without risking decompression sickness, and there was no way I could control Grandad's direction. Reluctantly I released my hold and the great ray passed beneath me. His huge wings stopped beating and he glided slowly away as if saying, "Hurry and catch up, I'll wait for you." For a moment I hung there motionless and with the slight buzz of nitrogen narcosis I imagined Grandad calling me to follow.

I began my ascent and watched Grandad disappear into the deep plankton layer. This would be our last day in the Sea of Cortez. In the evening the Baja Expeditions' *Don Jose* would return us to La Paz and we would fly back to the U.S. I found my way back to the seamount and resumed my grasp on the anchorline for decompression. As I waited for my meter to come out of the red, I noticed Marty Snyderman kneeling on the edge of the seamount—apparently waiting for Grandad to return one more time. Somehow I knew he wouldn't be back this afternoon and tomorrow we would be gone. I relaxed, closed my eyes, and tried to memorize emotions I had experienced during my flight into fantasy.

HOWARD HALL

Night of the Squid

T he ocean was perfectly still on this cold, moonless night in February. As our small boat rounded the west end of California's Catalina Island we could see the squid fishing fleet at anchor two miles away; their powerful fishing lights pushing out against the almost total darkness. So calm and dark was the night that the island and the sea could be distinguished from the sky only by a lack of stars. The squid fishing fleet looked like 14 brilliant fireflies suspended in space.

We approached one of the fishing boats and could see it was surrounded by a huge glowing mass of squid nearly 50 yards in diameter. Squid are often attracted to artificial lights and during the breeding season the lights not only attract them, but seem to enhance their courtship activity. The fishermen were busy dipping their six foot diameter brail net into the writhing mass and winching aboard incredible quantities of the seven to ten inch long cephalopods. In two hours they would take over ten tons. At the edge of the fishermen's pool of light, and passing through the periphery of the school, were numerous pilot whales and sea lions. And, knifing directly through the school, right beneath the brail net, were 20 or 30 large blue sharks.

The sharks were the reason we had come. Photographer

Marty Snyderman and I were working on a television special about sharks for National Geographic. Along with Bob Johnson, a marine naturalist and curator of the Cabrillo Marine Museum, and Jennifer Carter, associate producer for National Geographic Television, we had traveled to Catalina specifically to film the predation on squid by blue sharks. But as I watched the scene surrounding the fishing boat, I realized this was more than just a scene of predation. We were witnessing the culmination of the life cycle of an entire population of squid. They had come up from the dark depths of the sea to mate, lay their eggs, and die. It was a major event in the marine environment and one that did not go unnoticed by a large variety of the ocean's inhabitants.

The scene directly below the squid boat looked rather intense. The sharks were so engrossed in eating squid that I feared they might accidentally bite a diver in the process. Consequently, we tied our boat off 100 yards behind the fishermen, where the squid and sharks were less dense. It was decided that Marty and I would make the first dive alone and that Bob and Jennifer would follow later.

We dropped over the side of our boat and the ocean exploded in a brilliant flash of green bioluminescence. We descended 20 feet, swimming down through the almost total darkness toward our underwater movie lights, hanging on a power cable. Suddenly the darkness was penetrated by a blinding flash as Jennifer switched on the generator and the movie lights came to life.

Surrounding us were thousands of pulsating squid; their colors fluctuating in flashes from creamy white to reddish brown. Ignoring our presence, individuals searched frantically for mates. Below us the dark water flashed with green light as thousands of the arrow shaped creatures shot up toward our

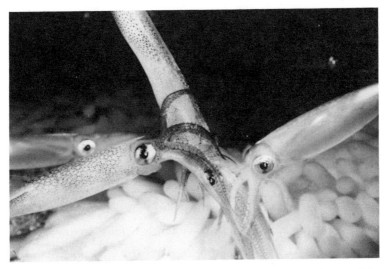

In the early spring, millions of squid come up from the dark depths of the sea to mate. Photo by Howard Hall.

movie lamps. After entering our tiny pool of light, couples would grasp each other and begin frenzied courtship.

During mating, the squid ignore their surroundings. This is their one chance in life to find a mate and ensure the perpetuation of their genetic code. I watched in rather morbid fascination as an occasional shark passed through the school devouring the mating pairs. Only two feet in front of my face an especially large blue shark grasped the tail of the female of a mating pair. Instead of releasing its dying mate and fleeing as the shark casually drew the pair into its maw, the male held fast until it, too, was consumed.

But, this desperate behavior makes sense in the world of the squid. They live only one year. And, during that time they roam the deep sea, growing, developing, and maturing in preparation for this one night. It's the most important night of their lives, and it's also their last. For after the males mate and the females lay their eggs, they all die. So it's understandable that on this night the squid have no fear of death, whether it be in the slashing jaws of the sharks or alone on the seafloor waiting for their rapidly degenerating bodies to cease functioning.

The night is also special for the sharks. If ever sharks dream, this must be a dream come true. So numerous are the squid and so unconcerned are they with their surroundings that the sharks can effortlessly consume mouthful after mouthful. One blue shark passed me with an enormously distended belly. It grabbed six or seven squid as it passed, then suddenly stopped, and while shaking its head back and forth violently, vomited out about 20 pounds of the dead cephalopods. After the spasm passed, the shark swam forward and began filling its belly again.

As we descended to 110 feet, a huge white cloud became visible in our lights. We had reached the bottom. But the ocean floor was invisible. It was entirely covered by the eggs of the squid.

The female squid produces an egg case that is nearly half the size of her body. The first squid to lay her eggs anchors the egg case to the sand by digging head first deep into it until only her undulating tail fins protrude. After the anchor has been placed, the squid digs herself out and leaves the creamy white and translucent egg case suspended above the sand. Soon the entire seafloor is covered with eggs and squid begin anchoring their egg cases to the anchors of earlier arrivals. At times the bottom is covered with eggs several feet deep and as far as a diver can swim in any direction.

Each egg case holds about 200 individual eggs. After a week the maturing embryos with their bright red eyes can be seen clearly by a diver if he/she holds a hand light behind the translucent case. After two weeks the eggs hatch and the tiny

While the squid are mating, they are oblivious to predators–animals such as blue sharks feast upon them until they are unable to eat more. Photo by Howard Hall.

squid venture out into deeper water to begin the cycle anew.

The egg-covered plain was a flurry of activity. Here the predation on the squid was even easier than below the fishing boat. Not only do the squid mate and lay eggs with complete disregard for numerous predators, but after the mating and egglaying the squid die. The process is not unlike the rapid aging and dying of salmon when they spawn. After mating and laying their eggs, male and female squid cease to be the quick, darting creatures that instantly flash from one color to another. Their bodies quickly begin to degenerate; their long sleek tentacles become twisted and disfigured and their color becomes a constant ghostly white.

The dying squid offer little resistance to the predators.

Numerous species of fish, crab, lobster, and several non-pelagic species of sharks, such as angel sharks and horn sharks, find capture of these failing bodies effortless. But, even with the mass gathering of these predators for this event, not to mention the heavy predation on the squid by man, they died faster than they could be taken. Soon the bottom was littered with their tiny corpses. In some places the dead squid lay in fields three and four feet deep.

Like the blue sharks, the smaller predators had eaten beyond their capacity. I watched as a comically swollen angel shark stared at a squid that was dying right in front of its face. I think the shark just wanted to sleep and rest its stomach, but the squid kept rolling up to its nose in the mild ocean surge. Finally, perhaps out of frustration or simply lack of self-control, the shark snapped up the squid. It chewed on the squid for awhile, alternating it from one side of its mouth to the other like a cigar. But, the shark couldn't swallow it. Finally the shark stopped moving and seemed to go back to sleep with the back half of the squid still sticking out of its mouth.

All the time Marty and I were down, our bright movie lights were attracting more and more squid. A sphere of squid accumulated around our lights like the large one that had developed around the squid boat. At times this became so dense we couldn't see more than two feet. We would have to swim hard for a few moments to get clear of the school. Blue sharks also noticed the high density of squid around the lights. Soon several of them were passing right before our cameras, preying on the school and providing excellent opportunities for filming. It wasn't long before the situation got out of control.

The number of blue sharks feeding on the squid surrounding our lights increased rapidly. The sharks would dash through the flashing mass, nictitating membranes covering their eyes, snapping out blindly for the inevitable mouthfuls of squid. Marty and I began to worry that the sharks might inadvertently bite one of us. When the shark action and density of squid became too great we would hastily swim out of the school.

But, soon the school was too large for us to find our way clear. The squid became so unbelievably dense they were getting into my mouthpiece and I could barely see the light coming from the powerful movie lamps I held in my hand. I felt something strike my left side and flinched. It may have been Marty accidentally kicking me but I wasn't sure. Then I was struck hard in the head and I saw the face of a shark, its teeth slashing as it gobbled squid just inches from my facemask. I didn't like the idea of swimming back to our boat in total darkness, but the alternative of staying with the lights and being the center of attention had become intolerable.

I dropped the lights and they immediately disappeared into the school. Marty had his hand on my tank, so he instantly (and thankfully) realized what I had done and in the darkness we raced skyward. We were bumped several more times before we cleared the school, but soon we were in the open and could slow our ascent rate. It was like being in a cold black closet. At first I couldn't even see the rim of my facemask. But soon, when my eyes began to adjust, I could see Marty's fiery green outline in the darkness as his movements disturbed the bioluminescent plankton. Then, I began to see thousands of streaks of green fire in the water. It was like being in the upper atmosphere on the edge of space during a great meteor shower. All around us brilliant arrows fired down from above. I paused for a moment for a last look at this ethereal scene and watched as thousands of squid rained down from above toward the ocean floor to mate, lay their eggs, and end their one year of life.

Playing Tag
with Wild Dolphins

t had been four years since I last knelt on the white sand of the Bahamas Banks listening for the calls of wild spotted dolphins. In the silence, looking out across the empty, sandy plain, I couldn't help feeling pessimistic. It seemed so very unlikely they would come racing from miles away to have a visit with me. It was not typical behavior for wild animals. But, then again, this was not a typical situation.

Hardy and Julia Whitty-Jones were more confident. They had been returning to the banks every year for nearly a decade. Every year the dolphins had been there and the relationship between humans and wild dolphins had grown from mutual curiosity to something that may approach mutual friendship. I had been along on several of the earlier expeditions to photograph the school for a film the Jones' would produce. In those early years the dolphins had been curious, but tentative. The encounters had been infrequent and brief. But Hardy and Julia explained that much has changed since my last dive with the "Spotters." Many members of the school had grown up having regular summer encounters with divers.

I heard the clicks and whistles. Moments later they surrounded me. The dolphins immediately came in much closer than in years past and moved with less trepidation. Nearest to me was a mother and her young calf. The baby was a beautiful and perfect miniature of her mother. She looked almost artificial. In years past the mothers never brought their calves in so close. It was as if this one was proudly showing off her baby. Suddenly I understood why. The top half of the mother's dorsal fin was missing. I couldn't believe it! It was Chopper, a dolphin we had seen eight years earlier when she was only a juvenile. Now she was an adult and had a calf of her own. She was one of many dolphins I would recognize from earlier times.

Julia swam over my shoulder carrying a bright red scarf. She dropped the scarf and swam back toward me. Then, just as the dolphins noticed it, Julia swam quickly back, grabbed the scarf, and made a big show of swimming away with it. The dolphins caught on fast. The next time Julia dropped the scarf the dolphins gave her no chance to retrieve it. A group of 20 or more rushed toward the scarf and the fastest one caught it on his pectoral fin. Somewhat less quickly than the animals, I realized we were playing "keep away." Julia, Hardy, several other divers, and I spent the next ten minutes trying to take the scarf from the dolphins. Of course, our swimming skills were non-existent compared to theirs, but they compensated by bringing the scarf to within inches of our fingertips.

The dolphin carrying the scarf would pass it from nose, to pectoral fin, to tail flukes with remarkable dexterity even while swimming at high speed. When a dolphin released the scarf, the other members of the group would compete for it at their top speed. Every time the scarf was dropped, we divers would go for it as fast as we could. This effort would have been futile except the dolphins seemed to have given us a handicap and would

Making allowances for their slower human playmates, the dolphins drop the scarf in front of a diver and wait for him to grab it. Photo by Howard Hall.

occasionally let one of us win. Once I even managed to take the scarf off the dolphin's pectoral fin! This was a remarkable demonstration of their physical control since the dolphins never permitted me to actually touch them.

I soon realized the dolphins had established rules to the game. Once a dolphin had the scarf it was his/hers until he/she chose to pass it on. No other dolphin would take it. Other dolphins would rub up against the scarf as it was carried by another, or even bite it, but it was against the rules to take it until released. Once released it was up for grabs, but it seemed understood that occasionally the divers should be given a turn.

We played "keep away" for nearly four hours. Although the dolphins seemed to be just warming up, we were exhausted. We swam back to the boat; trying to ignore the scarf that was being

Once the dolphins get used to having divers around, they go about their daily activities as if their visitors weren't there. The dolphins hunt for food, nurse their young and play games. Photo by Howard Hall.

trailed on a dolphin's tail flukes right before our noses. The dolphins finally departed as the last diver dragged himself up on the swim step. As I watched the school swim away, silhouetted against the white sand below the boat, one dolphin broke away, turned and swam back toward the boat. It made a quick pass by the swim step to drop off the red scarf.

In the weeks that followed the dolphins allowed me to swim with them as they hunted for food, nursed their young, and played games among themselves. Often juveniles would repeat the "keep away" game using a frond of seaweed. At the time I felt rather pleased we had managed to teach the dolphins a new pastime. But in retrospect, I'm not so sure they would see it that way. Dolphins with brains as large and as complex as our own have lived on this planet millions of years longer than we. It's quite possible the dolphins believe they taught us the game. And, I'm not sure they wouldn't be right.

Mugged by a Squid

Perhaps you were driving home one New Year's Eve, and a guy in the opposite lane woke up just before crossing the double yellow line. You may have been that close. On the very edge of the abyss. And you never knew it.

Was I on the very edge, or was I completely safe? The question drifted through my mind as I turned the 1,300 watt movie lights aside and looked straight down the monofilament line as it descended into darkness. The lights were so bright the glare actually hindered vision. But the power was necessary for filming big animals underwater at night. I was hoping for big animals. And I hoped I was being imaginative and not stupid. In the natural history film business, the difference between being imaginative and being recklessly stupid can simply be whether or not things go your way.

Aboard the *Ambar III*, my dad was doubled over a big game fishing pole in cheerful agony. His back was near failure and he occasionally passed the pole off to Bob Cranston when his muscles began to spasm. I'd brought my mom and dad along on the Sea of Cortez expedition to work as "production assistants." Simple nepotism. They know nothing about natural history film production.

I had no idea what dad had on the other end of the line. But Mike McGettigan, owner of the *Ambar III*, had explained that if you caught something big, at night, in deep water, giant squid would sometimes follow it to the surface. Some Mexican fishermen had been seeing big squid in this area. When asked how big, they spread their arms as wide as possible and said "*Grande!*" One fisherman noticed our diving gear and asked if we intended to swim with the squid. When we said yes, he shook his head solemnly and said, "Not a good idea."

My eyes played tricks on me as I hung suspended in oppressive darkness staring down the fishing line. Startling shapes would begin to materialize and then suddenly vanish. Imagination. I wondered about what the fisherman had said. Maybe this wasn't such a good idea. I looked up toward the surface and could see three skipjack tuna hanging over the side of the *Ambar III* for the squid to feast upon should they come up. I didn't know if the squid were dangerous or not. I'd never seen a Humboldt squid. But I knew of other things that hunted in deep, dark waters that were attracted to bleeding tuna. I'd forgotten my anti-shark suit. Left it at home in San Diego. Not a good idea at all.

A large shape materialized in the dark water below. In an instant I knew this one was real. After almost two hours of fighting, dad was about to reel in a 14 foot bigeye thresher shark. The lure had snagged the shark in the tail. I surfaced and tried to make myself heard over the whopping and hollering. "Let it go. I'll try to get a shot of it as it swims away," I yelled. Then I dropped back down to 30 feet and waited for the shark to be set free.

Alex Kerstitch jumped in with his still camera and grabbed a few shots of the shark before he began working to free the lure. While he was working, instinct induced me to look down.

Flashing! There were objects far below and they were flashing as if someone down there had a rapid fire strobe going off about five times a second! As the shapes ascended, I could see they were squid. The largest squid I'd ever seen!

A squid rushed past me and attacked the head of the thresher shark! The squid was about five feet long, a small one as this species of squid go. Humboldt squid reach 13 feet and 300 pounds! As it grasped the face of the shark, the squid began flashing from bright red to ivory white. It almost hurt my eyes. After a moment it let go of the shark and descended like a falling bomb.

Another, much larger squid rocketed past me. It grabbed a four foot long needlefish that was swimming just below the surface. The squid was more than five feet long and probably close to 70 pounds. As it descended with the needlefish, it began tearing it apart, leaving a cloud of blood and scales in its wake.

Alex unhooked the shark, and it dropped past me. I made a half conscious effort at filming it and botched the shot. Alex then swam out toward the squid that was ripping apart one of the skipjacks we had set out as bait. Squid were rushing past me. Most were in the 40 or 50 pound class. Some may have approached six feet and 100 pounds or more.

Something grabbed me from behind, and for a moment I could feel water rushing by as I was pulled back and down. I twisted around and saw the squid that had grabbed me rush away. I'd been pulled down about ten feet. I swam back to 30 feet and neutralized my buoyancy. I didn't take the time to consider what might have happened if the squid hadn't let go, or if more than one squid had grabbed me, or if a really big one had...

Everything seemed to be happening too fast. I still hadn't captured a single good shot. Every time I turned toward the squid with the movie lights, they descended and vanished. I

In the summer of 1990, juvenile jumbo squid–four to six feet long–rode unusual currents north from Brazil. A number of them ended up in the Sea of Cortez. These animals not only have nasty dispositions but are naturally equipped to do serious damage to those who cross their paths. Photo by Howard Hall.

suddenly realized it was the lights. They didn't like the lights! That was going to make filming them very difficult.

I wanted to film a squid attacking a free-swimming fish. But seeing how they avoided the movie lights, I decided to film one of the squid that was feeding on the skipjack bait. An enormous six foot squid had engulfed one of the baitfish and was tearing it apart. I swam over and began shooting. The squid fed so aggressively that it refused to leave its prey even when the lights were inches away. Blood and scales flew from the cluster of arms as they ripped at the fish.

I shot a variety of close-ups and then decided to get better acquainted. I reached out to touch the animal and was startled as a large, fleshy arm shot out and grabbed my hand. I jerked away and winced. Blood beaded on the back of my hand. This was not like handling an octopus! Alex had warned us that the big squid had sharp hooks that surrounded each powerful sucker disk. Not only does the sucker grab, but it also digs into the flesh. I was not curious enough to try it again.

Alex was behind me in the darkness. He had no movie lights to ward off the squid. A group ascended from the depths below, frenzied by the smell of blood in the water. Three large squid grabbed Alex at the same time. Suddenly, he felt himself rushing backward and down. A tentacle reached around his neck and ripped off his pre-Columbian gold pendant and chain, tearing the skin on his neck. Another squid ripped his decompression computer off his pressure gauge. Tentacles tore his dive light from his wrist and his collection bag off his waist. Then, as suddenly as they had grabbed him, the squid were gone.

When I got back on board, Alex had already gone to bed. He hadn't mentioned anything about the incident to the rest of the crew, and I hadn't seen it happen. So we continued to dive most of the night. We thought it strange that Alex had quit so early, though. He loved to night dive.

The squid mugging hadn't really terrified Alex while it was happening. He was too busy to be afraid. But when he got back on board, he began to wonder what if.... What if they had held on just a little longer? In moments they might have dragged him down into the abyss. What if they had ripped out his regulator? And his worst fear, what if the beak (much larger than a parrot's beak) had grabbed his neck and ripped out a two pound hunk of flesh? As he thought about it, his knees became progressively weaker. He decided he needed some rest.

KATHERINE GREEN

A writer whose credits include such television shows as "Taxi," "Cheers," and "Married . . . with Children," Kathy Green is looking forward to receiving an Emmy—although she hasn't yet been nominated for one. She is an Oklahoma native who claims she "moved to California after discovering that mattresses and chairs can, indeed, be strapped to the hood of your car." Kathy "now lives and writes in Los Angeles with her dog and editor, Tuffy."

KATHERINE GREEN

Wetsuit Squeeze— Delirious Deliberations of a Single Diver

I used to be just another young, single woman with a certain amount of animal magnetism. But, now that I'm a certified diver, I'm more than that. Now, I'm a woman of the '80s and can throw diving lingo around with the best of them. In fact, it's hard for me to believe there was a time I'd never uttered such phrases as "Where are my booties?" "Stop it, that's my dump valve," and "Yes, this is my weightbelt, was that your toe?"

But, as bizarre fate would have it, it turned out I'd made my first diving mistake years before, when I took up swimming laps in my apartment's pool.

Even though the pool was less than Olympic size, I was still able to successfully complete a good workout once I learned the best stroke count for small pools. It's One, two three, concussion. One, two, three, concussion. My biggest problem turned out to be the difference of opinion between me and the apartment manager as to what constituted a "heated pool." I believe a pool should be womb temperature. He felt swimming with an ice pick builds character. But, the solution soon came to me—in a dream,

I believe. I'll buy a wetsuit! Of course, I didn't know the exact term was wetsuit at the time. What I decided to buy was one of those rubber thingies people who swim in the ocean wear. So I did.

The clerk told me the suit should fit tight or it wouldn't work, so with some trepidation I bought a shortie that I could barely peel off after each swim. In fact, pulling the suit on and off soon became so much of a nuisance I abandoned the experiment and the colorful little rubber thingie disappeared into my closet.

That was five years ago. And, in those five years several incredible things happened. I earned enough money to buy a house and I discovered the fascinating and darn near affordable sport of diving. For a sniveling (albeit fashionable) coward such as myself this was quite a coup. But, in a decade where Michael Jackson can become a sex symbol, anything is possible.

Now, as everyone who's ever been involved with diving knows, it opens up a whole new world for the adventurous—the world of rentals! Rented tanks, rented regulators, rented weights. Ah! But after that open water class is completed and you become a "professional" amateur diver, that's when you take your first real plunge. Yes, the inevitable lure of owning my own custom gear soon grabbed me like nitrogen narcosis. I decided I'd buy everything I'd need. No more rentals for me. So, as I sat one afternoon, drooling over the ads for customized wetsuits, hoping that they also looked that good on women with normal-sized chests, I suddenly remembered I already owned one—a shortie at least. I ran from closet to closet hoping against hope. Question after question raced through my mind—did I still have it? Could I still find it? Can the White Sox win the pennant? Then, like magic, there it was—tucked behind the ski pants I wore once, back when I was a skier instead of a skin diver.

I took the wetsuit off the hanger and looked at it with a discriminating eye for the first time. Sure, I used to think it was a pain to get into and out of, but that was before my diving instructor had explained that pain and torture were fun. I threw off my clothes, unzipped the wetsuit and stepped in.

As I pulled the shortie up over my knees, it began to give less and less. But, I persisted. I plunged each arm into an armhole and tried to pull the suit up over my back. But, no dice. It lodged up around my shoulder blades and refused to move. I suddenly felt a sensation I'd never had before—not in the baggy rental suits I'd worn or even in this suit when I first bought it.

The blood vessels in my arms began to constrict. Could it be over the years this suit had shrunk? Could it be I had grown somewhat larger? As my legs began to grow numb, I summoned my good judgment and decided to take the thing off. I tried to pull my right arm out. It wouldn't budge. I tried my left arm. No luck. Both were wedged solidly in the sleeves. I was so constricted I couldn't raise either arm up far enough to help pull the other one free. I was stuck.

I began to whirl around the room, twisting and turning. The circulation in both arms was now completely cut off. I struggled a few seconds more, those inevitable thoughts racing through my mind; had anyone ever died from being stuck in a wetsuit? Could the White Sox win the pennant? I was getting delirious.

Different people have different fears. Some fear being trapped in elevators. Some fear being buried alive. I've always had a fear of being rolled up in a shag carpet. But that story is for the medical journals.

In a last ditch effort to resist further panic, I scoured my brain for an answer. I could remember nothing in my diver's manual about what to do if you got trapped inside a size six wetsuit.

The last thought I remember having were those of my own chastisement. Why had I moved to a house where no one could hear my cries for help? Why had I never married? Sure, I knew none of the men I'd ever dated were good enough. But, right now, even a pot-bellied, toothless, liquored up two-timer could've found scissors and cut me free, even if I had to promise him dinner.

I was growing too weak to care anymore when suddenly I heard the front door open. I recognized the voice. My sister had decided to drop by. Trying to look as dignified as possible, I waddled into the other room and hurriedly asked her to help me out of the wetsuit. As she began to pry my arms loose from this suction suit, I distinctly heard her muffle a laugh. Now that my panic had subsided, I found new room for anger. I started to make a snide remark like, shut up. But as one arm sprang free, my good nature returned. Why get upset with a mere sibling who hated water so much she'd never even learned to swim? How unfair to expect someone like that to understand the daredevil world of the diver.

BOB TALBOT

Those who have seen a Bob Talbot poster are unlikely to forget it. The mammals he photographs above or below the water express energy and enjoyment of their world. Some appear to be viewing the camera with a mixture of curiosity and benevolence.

A Southern California resident, Talbot began snorkeling at age 8 and became a certified scuba diver at age 13. He acquired a camera at age 14, which led to an interest in marine photography. He is not only an immensely gifted still photographer but a cinematographer as well. His photography has been published in numerous books and magazines. His film work has been included in several TV presentations by the Cousteau Society.

In 1992 Bob produced and directed a video, *Dolphins and Orcas*. A fluid feast for the senses, it consists of unbelievably beautiful and mostly slow motion footage of dolphins and killer whales set to music.

Committed to the protection and preservation of the species he photographs, Talbot is involved with a number of environmental groups.

Whale of a Rescue

On the morning of January 4, 1985, my friend Jeff Kornmann and I were out on my 25 foot Skipjack *Holdout*. At about 8:30AM we were just past Dana Point (California) heading north when we heard a call over the marine radio to the Coast Guard from the fishing vessel *Pronto*. They had come across a gray whale entangled in a gill net, and were requesting assistance. We made contact with the *Pronto* and headed out to its position approximately 11 miles offshore.

On our arrival we were discouraged to see that the whale was completely wrapped in the net, with a large mass of net and five buoys gathered at the tail. Jeff tended the boat while I entered the water with a cutting tool improvised by the crew of the *Pronto*. Underwater, the situation was even worse than it appeared from the surface; the whale, which was approximately 35 feet long, was wrapped in three or four layers of net, along with lengths of one-half inch polypropylene and three-eighths inch nylon lines. The whale seemed agitated by my presence and did what it could to avoid me.

It was obvious that the problem required more than one diver, so I returned to my boat and notified the *Pronto* that we would stay with the whale until more help arrived.

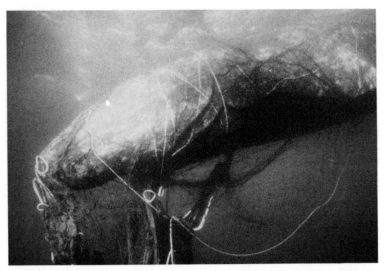

Upon getting into the water with a 35-foot whale, the divers find it wrapped in three or four layers of net, along with lengths of half-inch polypropelene and 3/8 inch nylon lines. The animal seems agitated by the divers' presence. Photo by Bob Talbot.

The *Pronto* left, and we radioed the Coast Guard for assistance. After about a half hour we made contact, and brought them up to date. There is, apparently, no set procedure for a live cetacean tangled in a net, and so we were left to stand by for a lengthy stretch of time while the Coast Guard figured out what to do. Finally they informed us that the R/V *Westwind*, with personnel from MBC Applied Environmental Sciences aboard, would join us in approximately three hours.

At about 1:30PM the *Westwind*, accompanied by the Dana Point Surfwatch boat, arrived. On board the *Westwind* were MBC personnel Larry Nufer (captain); Lori Nufer (mate); Charles T. Mitchell, Sr. (deck); Kathryn Mitchell (photographer); Chuck Mitchell, Rick Ware, and Michael Sowby (marine biologists–divers). Aboard the *Surfwatch* was Gary Harvey (boat operator);

Mike Broussard (lifeguard); Ted Ehrheart (ranger); Jeff Kirkpatrick (park aide); and David K. Johnson (National Marine Fisheries Service special agent).

Mitchell and Ware approached the whale in a small inflatable boat to review the situation and after a brief discussion it was decided that Chuck Mitchell, Ware, Sowby, and Broussard, using only snorkeling gear, would attempt to cut the whale free. I entered the water with a small scuba tank and camera to obtain underwater photos.

The whale was swimming at approximately 0.5 to 1 knot as the divers slowly cut away the net. After taking several photographs, I decided I would be more useful helping them cut, so I handed my camera up to one of the hands and moved toward the whale's head. The others had realized that working near its head excited the whale, and they had moved back. I had been busy taking pictures and I didn't realize this. I swam to the right side of the whale's head, held onto one of the polypropylene lines, and began sawing through it. The whale reacted, and began shaking its head back and forth, but I hung on and kept cutting, figuring we'd have to get to the head eventually. As the whale's movements became powerful, I decided I'd better let go, only to find that I, too, had become entangled.

I reached back to try to unsnag my tank valve. The whale was thrashing all this time, making it very difficult for me to do anything. The more it thrashed, the more entangled I became. Soon I realized I needed help, and when the whale surfaced I called out to the other divers.

I was pulled down again. Trying to cut myself free with one hand, I held onto my regulator with the other. I was getting winded, and I knew if I lost my regulator, I'd be in real trouble. The net was snagged on my mask and regulator, but I was able

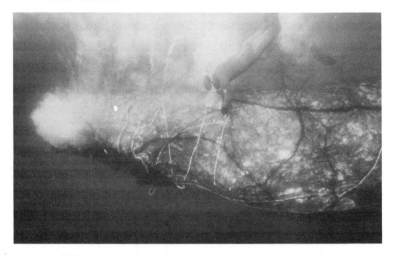

Rick Ware holds onto the gill net and continues cutting it as the whale dives.
Photo by Bob Talbot.

to free the regulator. This continued for what seemed like a few minutes, while Chuck Mitchell was trying to get to me and to release the shoulder strap on my backpack. I had a rubber sleeve over the strap and it was difficult to get it undone. Finally he got it to the point where I could slip out of it. I was hesitant to let go of the tank, not knowing whether or not I was still tangled, but had little choice.

I let the pack go, surfaced, and felt a tug at my legs. My fins were still caught in the net. I yelled out, "My fins!" just as I was pulled under. I was able to kick off my left fin, but my leg was wrapped in the line and I couldn't get out of my right fin. Chuck dove down and was able to cut the line around my leg and free my right fin. I was helped aboard the inflatable from the *Westwind* and transported to the *Surfwatch*. From that point on, I watched from the *Surfwatch* boat, feeling frustrated and embarrassed.

It was decided that Mitchell and Ware would continue the cutting, with Broussard and Sowby standing by. A half inch nylon rope was attached to some trailing rope and netting, then secured to the *Westwind* in hopes of restricting the whale's movement. This proved ineffective, and resulted in the whale towing the vessel, stern first, into prevailing seas at about two knots.

By about 3:30 most of the body had been cleared, with only the head and the flukes still tangled. The head was freed by attaching a buoyed line to the net around the snout, which the *Surfwatch* towed forward, slipping it free.

With most of the whale free of the net, it became much more vigorous, making it impossible to approach the tail and the remaining net. The *Westwind* contacted Hubbs/Sea World for advice, but they were unable to give any suggestions. From the inflatable, Mitchell and Ware tried repeatedly to secure to the net, in an attempt to at least remove some of the buoys. This resulted in Ware's being thrown from the boat when it was hit by the flukes. Upon its impact with the inflatable, the whale rushed forward, snapping the trailing line. With daylight fading, it was decided that no further attempts would be made to free the whale. Trailing approximately 20 feet of net and five buoys, the whale swam off in a WNW direction.

The following Wednesday the whale was sighted again off Santa Cruz Island. National Park Service and Navy divers jumped from a helicopter in another attempt to free the whale. The whale reacted in much the same way as it had with us, and the divers were able to remove only one of the buoys. Amazingly, my mask, tank and fin were still caught in the net.

The last reported sighting of the whale was off Santa Rosa Island.

The gill net problem facing whales and other marine life is a serious one. According to Carol Pillsbury, manager of the Channel Islands Marine Sanctuary, in the first five weeks of 1985 alone there were helicopter sightings of five whales (three grays, two humpbacks) caught in nets. At present there is an extensive stranding program to deal with dead cetaceans, but no organized program to deal with live whales caught in nets. I urge the American Cetacean Society and other interested groups to become involved in organizing such a program in cooperation with the National Marine Fisheries Service.

The gill net controversy is an old one, but one that has not until recently gained much media attention. Our episode received considerable coverage in newspapers and on television. Unfortunately, all but one of the stories centered on me being entangled in the net. The fact of the matter is that the only reason I was stuck in the net was because I made an error in judgment that I'm not at all proud of. Chuck Mitchell, who cut me out of the net, along with Rick Ware, did the most to help the whale, and got the least recognition. The stories were misquoted, exaggerated, and melodramatic. Although I'm glad this incident has brought attention to the gill net problem, it's disappointing that it took a person being endangered to get the story out.

Every year thousands of marine animals are subject to slow, painful deaths in gill nets. A large portion of these catches are "incidental" and the animals are simply killed and thrown over the side. This has been going on for years, although it was not readily recognized by the press until a human life was at risk. Perhaps the mistake is one we're making as a species, by allowing thousands of animals to suffer and die each day—not only in gill nets, but in countless other ways as well. We as individuals cannot count on the six o'clock news to learn what is going on. We must learn by whatever means are accurate and fair, and use this knowledge to help in whatever ways we can.

I have been asked many times if I thought the whale knew

we were trying to help it. From its reaction, I sincerely doubt it. It was a trapped, frightened animal and our approach probably posed a threat. In reality, man is a threat. Ours is the species that brought the gray whale to the brink of extinction, the species that, under the guise of "loving" whales, invades its migratory path with fleets of boats, and the species that set adrift the very net in which the whale was entangled.

There is much discussion as to what agency, group, or organization should be responsible for these problems. We are all responsible, and we need to work together to find the solutions.

RICHARD ELLIS

The foremost painter of marine natural history subjects in America, Richard Ellis is also a prolific author. He has written (and illustrated) five books. More than 80 magazine articles and several screenplays on whales also bear his byline. In search of undersea subjects he has traveled all over the world; many of the places he has been will be visited by most divers only in their imaginations. Ellis's paintings are very realistic, showing details it would be impossible to photograph.

Ellis is a trustee of the Oceanic Society and a special adviser to the American Cetacean Society. He is a member of the Explorers Club, the Society for Marine Mammalogy, and the

New York Academy of Sciences. He has been a member of the U.S. delegation to the International Whaling commission since 1980.

RICHARD ELLIS

A Bigger Fish Story

There are numerous authenticated cases of great white sharks attacking people in the water. People often die as a result of these attacks, making *Carcharodon carcharias* the most feared animal in the sea. Other sharks attack people, but the size and strength of the great white make it so ominous and terrifying that no other species can compete with it for instilling raw fear.

Despite its name, the white shark is not really white, but dark yellowish-gray above, and dirty white below. The lobes of its tail are almost equal in size, unlike those of most other species, where the upper lobe is considerably longer than the lower. White sharks are further characterized by a black spot at the base of the pectoral fins. The nose is pointed, the teeth triangular and serrated, and the eyes are black and apparently pupilless.

In *Jaws*, the white shark dining off the New England coast is described by the shark-hunting Captain Quint as being 20 feet in length. There then follows a discussion of how long these sharks are known to grow, and ichthyologist Hooper says, "people generally accept 30 feet as maximum size, but the figure is fancy." Documented records support the ichthyologist. No white shark longer than 21 feet has ever been accurately measured, and even this figure is open to question.

The dreaded great white shark has a pointed nose, triangular, serrated teeth, and black, apparently pupilless eyes. Painting by Richard Ellis.

Henry Bigelow and William Schroeder make note of this 21-foot beast in their book *Fishes of the Western North Atlantic.* "We have received a good photograph, apparently of this specimen, with weight stated at 7,302 pounds, from Ollyandro del Valle." The authors never saw the specimen and relied on information received from a Cuban ichthyologist, Luis Howell-Rivero. In 1974, while preparing *The Book of Sharks,* I tried to locate the "good photograph" but a copy of it could not be found.

Three years later I received a photograph from underwater photographer Jerry Greenberg, with a note that he had gotten it from a Cuban diver. The photo showed a large white shark, surrounded by a group of people. Dario Guitart-Manday, another Cuban ichthyologist, sent me a copy of a paper he had written in 1975. In that paper he interviewed one of the fishermen who landed the 7,000 pound shark in 1945. In the article, I read that the shark was never actually weighed, but ". . . a knowledgeable fisherman guessed it weighed more than 7,000 pounds." How this estimate got translated into the precise figure of 7,302 pounds is a secret that is probably forever lost. One of its teeth is pictured in Guitart-Manday's paper and is just shy of three inches (7.5 cm) in length. I had originally thought this shark was pure fiction, but after seeing the photograph and the article, I could not be completely certain.

The largest white shark caught on rod and reel was a 2,664 pound female taken off the Australian coast in 1959. Larger great white sharks have been harpooned, including a 15 foot specimen weighing 3,301 pounds, and two other ton and a half animals taken off the California coast in 1975, when the *Jaws* mania was at its peak. On the wall of a saloon in Montauk, Long Island, there hangs the mounted head of an enormous white shark, harpooned by Capt. Frank Mundus. The label reads the shark was 17 and a half feet long, weighing 4,500 pounds.

In the summer of 1978 there were tales of a huge white shark off Montauk, Long Island. Fishermen were unable to harpoon the shark, but reported it was enormous. Jack Casey, shark expert from the Narragansett, Rhode Island, laboratory of the National Marine Fisheries Service, saw the photographs and said the shark was "over 20 feet, probably considerably larger than the largest on record, which is 21 feet."

June 1980. We were flying out of Montauk, looking for sperm whales earlier seen in the area. I was with Russ Kinne, pilot and wildlife photographer; Dr. Jay Hyman, a marine mammal veterinarian; and my wife. Flying at altitudes of 1,000 to 1,500 feet, we scanned the ocean. I spotted a strange disturbance in the distance, a V-shaped ripple as if something was being dragged along the surface. We banked the plane toward the movement in the water, and realized it was the wake made by the dorsal fin of a large shark.

The shark below was between 25 and 30 feet long. Familiar with sharks and whales, we felt we could estimate its size. Above the roar of the engine we all began to shout "white shark," and it appeared we had come upon the legendary "Montauk Monster" last seen in August 1978. We probably estimated its size correctly, but we didn't do as well when it came to species identification.

We came down to earth when our photographs were developed and sent to shark expert Casey. He said the pictures showed a basking shark, but even more significantly, the shark he identified (from aerial photographs only) as a white in 1978, (the "Montauk Monster"), was probably a basker as well. The small eyes and huge gill slits of the baskers are visible at sea level, but not from the air. Our shark also had strongly triangular pectoral fins, whereas the pectoral fins of whites are more sickle-shaped. Like so many others, we had been influenced by our desires: our mind's eye had turned harmless basking sharks into gigantic man-eaters.

RICHARD ELLIS

How to Paint a Whale

First you have to find one. With most other wildlife subjects, you can either go out and photograph the animal in the wild, or perhaps even find a suitable model in the zoo. There are, unfortunately for the aspiring whale artist, no whales in zoos or aquariums. (The only large whale ever kept in captivity was a juvenile gray whale that lived for a year at Sea World in San Diego, but had to be released because of the $1,000 a day feeding bill.) Even when you are lucky enough to see a whale from a boat, the chances are that you will see only a rolling, shiny back. Some whales breach, of course, but that is a difficult moment to capture, either on film or in your mind's eye, since it usually consists of a lot of splashing with a big black animal hidden somewhere in the foam, and more often than not, in exactly the opposite direction of the one you were looking.

If you can't see a whale in an aquarium or from a boat, how then can you have any idea at all about the animal's actual appearance? Whales live in the ocean, so the first step is to go into the ocean. (Of course, you must only go into the ocean where there are supposed to be whales; just swimming off Coney Island or Malibu is not going to produce much in the way of subject matter.) So the first order of business is to find out where the whales are. The best way to do that would be to avail yourself of a copy of *The Book of Whales*, written and illustrated by that eminent whale-painter and cetologist, R. Ellis. This book will not only tell you where to look for Tasmanian beaked whales and pygmy right whales, but it will also tell you, as the student wrote in his report, "more than you want to know about whales."

You would learn, for example, that there are humpbacks off Hawaii or Massachusetts, gray whales off California (Alta and Baja) and Alaska, and right whales off Maine and Patagonia. So all you have to do is go to Hawaii, Massachusetts, California (Alta and Baja), Alaska, Maine, or Patagonia, and jump in the water, right? Well, no. It is against the law to even get close to a whale (or a sea lion, dolphin, or sea otter) in U.S. waters without a permit. So you either get a permit—for which you have to be a scientist with a damn good reason to want to get close to your subject—or you go to a place where they don't require permits. Like Patagonia.

To get to Patagonia, which is in southern Argentina, you have to convince the Argentine government that you are a Good Person, and that your trip will somehow benefit *them*. (Governments are like that.) You have to promise to write magazine articles and do paintings, show evidence that someone is going to print the former and buy or publish the latter, and then you actually have to *do* it—but I am getting ahead of my story. You have to get on an airplane with all your cameras, wetsuits, and other paraphernalia, and then fly for 14 hours to Buenos Aires. And that's only the beginning of the trip. From B.A. you fly in a small plane to Trelew, rent a car, and drive for another four hours to Puerto Pyramides. Now you are ready to look for whales.

The first southern right whale I ever saw was cavorting in the bay at Pyramides. There wasn't much to see from shore (just a rolling, shiny back and a plume of spray where the whale had exhaled), so we had to launch a small boat to get us to the place where we could actually get in the water with the great whales. On this expedition, my diving companion (and liaison with the Argentine government, then being ruled by a military junta), was Ricardo Mandojana, an Argentine born physician, now stationed in Washington, D.C., who had dived many times before with the *Ballenas francas* of Peninsula Valdes. Two hundred yards from our boat, we saw our first whales. From sea level, they looked absolutely enormous; great glistening black humps, rolling and blowing in the choppy waters. We cut our motor so as not to spook the whales and dropped overboard as quietly as we could. The water temperature was about 48°F, so we wore full wetsuits, gloves, and neoprene boots. We both carried underwater cameras, hoping to capture the great leviathans on film. Swimming with whales that might be 50 feet long and weigh as many tons is a truly humbling experience; there is probably no sensation on earth like the feeling you get when you get close to a great whale. You suddenly realize what the words awesome, huge, and powerful *really* mean. And it is these words that describe not only the whales, but also the problems in photographing them. Yes, it is probably dangerous to be that close to that big an animal, even if the creature is a "gentle giant," but I am talking about photographic problems. Consider this: If you are close enough to a whale to see it clearly—remember that water is not nearly as good a medium for photography as air—then you can't get the whole whale in the picture and if you're far enough away to see the entire animal, then the water will interfere with your photography to such a great extent that all your pictures will be soft and hazy.

A painting of a right whale and calf. When he was underwater with these animals, the artist got close enough to see the barnacles and the whale lice on their skin. Painting by Richard Ellis. Photo by Robert E. Mates

But we did it anyway; we dived with the whales (and the dusky dolphins and the sea lions), for 6 of the 15 days we were in Patagonia. At one point we had to wait on shore and twiddle our thumbs for five straight days because the wind was blowing too hard for us to launch the boat. Because I would not know how well our photographs would come out, I tried to burn the images of the whales into my mind. I got as close to them as I could; close enough to see the barnacles and the whale lice on their skin; close enough to get tumbled when one of them raised its 18 foot tail flukes without knowing I was right behind it.

On shore, I tried to supplement my recollections with notes and sketches, trying to keep as accurate a record as I could of what I saw. When we got back to the U.S., practically the first thing I did was to take my film to be developed. I thought it was too risky to entrust it to any photo shop—they had lost an occasional roll before—so I drove it out to the Kodak lab in Fairlawn, New Jersey, and then went back the next day to pick it up. Some of my pictures were OK, but curiously enough, my desire to paint whales was supported by the mediocre quality of the photographs. (While I am not a world-class underwater photographer, Ricardo Mandojana is, and many of his shots have been published in major magazines, from *Natural History* to *Audubon*.) In order to show one of these giants in a proper setting, and in a position where non-cetologists can see what it really looks like, I believe that you have to paint it.

And so I began a series of Patagonian paintings, mostly of right whales, but also of the dolphins. I made sketch after sketch, using photographs and my own recollections. I painted one right whale near the bottom, and a mother and calf in deep water. I painted a whale with a flotilla of dusky dolphins, and also a single dolphin with a school of anchovies. I wrote articles about my experiences for *Science/80* (I had gone to Patagonia in 1979), *Oceans, Sport Diver, International Wildlife,* and *Americas,* thus discharging my debt to the Argentines who had financed my trip.

Even though there are now more and better photographs of whales than there were when I started my career as a whale painter, I still believe that the best way to show whales is to paint them. (In 1974, to illustrate an article in *Audubon* on the great whales, I did ten major whale paintings. In 1985, when I wrote the ten year "anniversary" follow-up to that article, there were enough photographs—some of them by my friend Mandojana— to make a new set of paintings unnecessary.) In the course of my

A painting of a right whale and dusky dolphins. The animals are so large that Ellis believes the only way to show the way they really look underwater is to paint them. Painting by Richard Ellis.

research, I have traveled to Japan (where I shipped aboard a whaling vessel), Alaska, the Azores, Hawaii, Mexico, Bermuda, the Galapagos, Australia, New Zealand and Newfoundland. I have painted every species of cetacean, and all the pinnipeds as well. Someone once asked me why I painted whales and I jokingly answered "because I can't do feet." In fact, I can do feet; I once drew a whole zoo full of terrestrial mammals for the Denver Zoological Gardens.

I paint whales for science as well as for art. But whatever the motivation, I don't paint them because they're easy. Oh yes, they have fairly simple shapes and they are not decorated with feathers, fur, or scales. It's not the shapes that are hard; it's the knowledge of what they look like. And I'm still learning.

CHRISTOPHER NEWBERT

Some of the finest underwater photographers in the world winced when they learned Chris Newbert was working on another book. This is because his first publication, *Within a Rainbowed Sea*, caused most of them to turn green with envy. It is a beautiful book, full of spectacular undersea images captured and described by Chris. It has garnered so many honors and awards there isn't space to list them all and still have room to tell you just a little about the man himself.

Newbert took up underwater photography in 1972. The first magazine to publish one of his photos was *Skin Diver* and he immediately became a regular contributor to Fish of the

Month, the magazine's photographic showpiece. Since then Newbert's work has appeared in 149 other publications.

Newbert is currently working on a book about the Red Sea. He and his wife, Deda, escort underwater photo tours to exotic locales several months of the year. In addition to diving, they love to ski.

CHRISTOPHER NEWBERT

Shark Attack!
... a love story

S hark. Say the word slowly, listening with care. Sshhark. It starts smoothly with a kind of swooshing noise, pleasing to the senses. It's almost tactile. You can feel the graceful power of the animal slicing effortlessly through the water, unimpeded by the dense fluid, as if flying through thin air, its long, powerful caudal fin tracing smooth continuous arcs on a three dimensional canvas. Like the animal's tail, the silky sound is long and drawn out as well, sweeping one forward, unsuspecting, until the word comes suddenly to its harsh, biting end ... sshhaaRK. How appropriate. How appropriate for the image this creature conjures in our collective consciousness. It is the perfect symbol of mindless evil, roaming unseen depths, violently striking carefree souls as they frolic innocently in the sea. It is an image brought to life in print and celluloid, and has made millions for the authors of these terrible visions. It is this image that so many of us have carried along to some extent during our first excursions under the sea, a dark, shadowy presence lurking just beneath the surface of our exhilaration and joy.

Years ago, like many neophyte divers, I wondered how I

might react to my first shark: Fear, panic, acceptance, bravado? In retrospect, my first shark experience was almost a non-event. Time has condensed this memory into a series of quick-cut images, as if some cerebral editor has excised most of the meaningless frames in this mental movie, leaving me with a series of significant stop-action pictures. The shark simply approached—cut! Stopped—cut! Looked at me—cut! And left. Cut. That was it and then I was left behind like a dissatisfied first-time lover, thinking, is that all there is?

Fortunately not. Having spent so many hours underwater since that time, the number and the excitement level of my shark encounters has increased dramatically. My initial curiosity concerning my reaction to these creatures has been resolved over and over, though often with different answers—answers spanning the emotional rainbow, from bright, sunny, and cheerful, to dark, foreboding, and fearful. Nevertheless, the shark encounter is like an addictive drug, and one craves the intensity of the experience in ever increasing amounts.

And of these many memories, one stands out with particular clarity, perhaps because my fear quotient was higher than normal. That, and the fact I was not at all frightened for myself.

I was working in the open ocean off the Kona Coast of Hawaii photographing schools of wild Pacific spotted dolphins. With me, and experiencing this bottomless environment for the first time, was my girlfriend, Deda. (Now her name is really Birgitte, but, like verbal sharks, Americans butcher the Danish pronunciation to such a degree she has chosen to go by her childhood nickname. For whatever good it has done. Even reduced to such a simple level, we in this country still can't get it. But she won't succumb, she won't change her name to Sue. Deda it is and Deda it will remain.)

Anyhow, my pre-dive briefing on working with these dolphins was somewhat lacking in the nastier potential aspects of this experience. Maybe I didn't want to frighten her. (I probably didn't want to frighten myself.) What I should have said, but didn't, was, keep your eyes peeled. Oceanic whitetip sharks are often found swimming with schools of marine mammals. By the way, I needed to add but again didn't, they get big, VERY BIG, and are known to be a bit ah, cranky. And I could have gone on about the difference between the tail motion of the dolphin (up and down) versus the shark (side to side) as being the first visual clue amid the chaos of hundreds of big gray swimming things speeding this way and that. But I didn't say any of this, as you now know. It was all sunshine and the glory of swimming with the sleek dolphins, wild and free. And of course, I was newly in love, so my whole world was sunshine, wildness, and freedom, as only one in love can feel.

And so it went. For a while at least. We chased dancing beams of light into the sparkling sea, pausing at depth to let these exquisite creatures glide around us, filling the ocean with whistles and song. It was euphoric. I was euphoric. Surely she was falling in love with me as well, or so I hoped. Oh Chris, you old shark, I smirked to myself, secretly pleased with my day's progress.

Then, having moved the boat to a new position in the school, we again slipped into the water (free diving only, in case you imagined otherwise). We drifted a considerable distance from my Boston Whaler, and had moved somewhat apart from each other. It's easy to get carried away when surrounded by hundreds of these beautiful, exuberant creatures. Finishing a dive, I broke the surface and looked toward the boat, now 100 feet away. An animal was coming toward me, but the tail was moving quickly from side to side. It was no dolphin. It was too big anyhow. The dolphins only get seven to eight feet max, and this guy had a foot or two on any of them.

I quickly looked toward Deda, but she was oblivious to this unfolding drama. She had never seen a shark before, not even the harmless little reef varieties, those often bitchy, always pretentious little pups with barely a legitimate claim to their honorable name. This was a good eight, maybe nine foot oceanic whitetip, a real shark, a varsity league shark, the kind of shark you may never learn to love, but you'll always respect the next morning. I raised my head out of the water, spit out my snorkel, cleared my throat and attempted to call her name without creating any undo alarm. "Ah, (gurgle, cough) . . . Deda . . . ahem, Deda!" I finally got her attention after several attempts. I pointed at the rapidly approaching shark with feigned confidence, but the best I could manage was, "It's not a dolphin!"

She was not impressed. Not with me, not with the shark. As it swam past, she attempted to grab its tail. Grab its tail?? Jeez! Do you know what that thing is? She didn't hear me. She was diving down again for a better, more intimate look as it swept past her, closer still. Horrible images filled my mind. Good lord, I thought. How will I explain this to her parents and I don't even speak a word of Danish? How will I send whatever's left back to Copenhagen? And where the hell is Copenhagen? I was really starting to take charge now.

Many ever-tightening circles and several near passes later, the lethal beast straightened its path and headed away. Overwhelmed with relief, I finally got Deda's attention once again and began to recite to her what would have been a more appropriately scheduled dissertation while still in the boat, before ever getting wet. But of course, at this point the whole world knows I didn't do that. So there we were, bobbing around in the open

While free diving in the Red Sea with Deda, Chris Newbert looks up to see an oceanic white tip shark headed right at him. Photo by Chris Newbert.

sea, miles from shore and I was explaining that this is arguably the most aggressive species of pelagic shark there is. That they, on occasion, *LIKE* human sashimi. Perhaps chasing their tails, I offered, is best left to experienced divers with some knowledge of the subtle mood swings and behavior patterns of such carnivores. She nodded at my words and I presumed she was taking to heart my note of caution. Such a large shark, I stressed with rising emotion, could easily masticate her. She slapped me hard, possibly misunderstanding.

With that, she looked below the surface and saw the shark speeding back straight at us. Grabbing a quick breath, she dived down and swam directly at the approaching beast. They were on a collision course and my heart was pounding. Then, extending her arms forward with fearless abandon, she grabbed the head of the shark and thrust the huge animal aside, her long blond hair flying outward as she was spun around, a matador's golden cape flourished in triumph.

Me? Oh. Well, I was doing my best to take a picture, ever the

After circling Chris and Deda several times, the shark straightens its path and heads away. Photo by Chris Newbert.

dedicated photographer. Besides, I felt marginally safer hiding behind my bulky camera housing. Unfortunately, I was shaking too badly to get much of a shot.

A year and many sharks later, she's still intact and still won't listen to me, both to her credit. I'm still in love by the way, more than ever, and I'm finally starting to get the pronunciation right. I may impress her yet.

JACK McKENNEY

Few people in the scuba world are as loved as was Jack McKenney. When he died at the age of 50 in 1988, the underwater world was shocked and greatly saddened. His movies, which brought him many awards and myriad avid fans, were filmed, directed, edited, and written by Jack. McKenney was also an accomplished still photographer and prolific author. His articles and photographs appeared in *Skin Diver* throughout his eight year stint as an editor there and afterward, when he left the magazine to work full time as an underwater cinematographer. Jack wrote one book, *Dive to Adventure*, published in 1983 by Panorama Publications, Inc.

Beneath the Sulu Sea

We had just surfaced in the middle of the Sulu Sea to an incredibly beautiful sunset. The water was like burnished pewter and reflected a flowered rose from the magnificent orb sinking into the horizon. I laid back on the surface, supported by the air in my buoyancy compensator and focused on a quarter moon riding high in the evening sky. My son John, Bob Abrams, and Pam Jordan were with me. We floated, cameras and lights in hand, marveling at the magnificent sight.

Anchored a quarter of a mile away was the *Lady of the Sea*, our boat and home for two weeks. Jimmy Dotimis, the very capable outboard mechanic and dive tender, was heading out in the dinghy to pick us up.

The 120-foot-long *Lady of the Sea* has an interesting history. She was built in 1962 as a British subchaser and later sold to President Sukarno of Jakarta, who used her as a yacht. Later she was sold to a Chinese gentleman who used it for smuggling for two years in the Philippines before the Coast Guard apprehended him. Then Theresa Jison and her partner Roger Imperio, a colonel in the Air Force, acquired the boat and turned it into a luxurious dive cruiser. Another version of the story is that Sukarno gave it to a favorite mistress who was an aunt or cousin of Theresa's family. In any case, Theresa took it over, brought Roger into the business, and together, after making extensive alterations, they had her operating as she was that day.

The previous year I had traveled to the Sulu Sea to produce a diving travel film in conjunction with Poseidon Travel Ventures and our hosts Gloria Maris and the Philippine government. I was so overwhelmed with the fantastic diving that I returned to lead a group of divers and to shoot more film, just for fun.

The Sulu Sea, roughly 1,200 miles long and 800 miles wide, is an exotic body of water that washes up against the main Philippine Islands of Palawan to the west, Mindoro to the north, and Panay and Negros eastward. In the left-hand corner is Borneo. Mindinao closes the gap on the southeast quadrant.

About 100 miles into the middle of the Sulu Sea from the island of Palawan are the Tubataha Reefs, comprised of the north and south reefs and Jessie Beazley reef. The latter was named after an English hydrographer. It's believed that Tubataha is actually the top of one of two submerged extinct volcanos. The inner lagoons are sand filled and encircled completely with coral, like an atoll.

Mariners must be cautious when sailing here for a couple of reasons: although there is a lighthouse on the southeast corner of the south reef, the light and batteries were stolen—so at night there is no indication the reefs are here. At low tide much of the reef breaks the surface. Also, modern-day pirates and smugglers frequent these waters. The *Lady of the Sea* is registered as a Coast Guard auxiliary cruiser; and early one morning when we were arriving at a new dive location a speed boat took off when its crew presumably saw the Coast Guard insignia on the side of the ship.

Half an hour earlier we had stepped off the stern of the *Lady* for a twilight dive. We were hoping to catch some of the whitetip

An aerial view of one of the Tubataha Reefs. Photo by Jack McKenney.

sharks settling down for the night in one or two of the numerous caves along the wall at the northeast corner of the north reef.

The current had been ripping and we tore along the wall at 120 feet looking for the caves the sharks frequented. During the filming of *Beneath the Sulu Sea,* which I had produced the previous year, Bob and I had filmed both whitetips and nurse sharks sleeping in these caves, so I wanted John and Pam to see them.

I had dropped to 140 feet, looked down into the twilight gloom and counted at least ten fairly large sharks scurrying about near the sloping bottom 30 feet deeper. Some of them seemed awfully big for whitetips, but I remembered there were big oceanic whitetips and bull sharks here, too. And big they were. One ten-footer shot up at me, made an inquisitive pass, then shot back down to the pack. I swam up to Pam and John just as they were looking into a cave. I filmed them slipping into the entrance, then ducked in myself. Immediately, off to the right, I spotted a six-foot whitetip, so I turned on my movie light and got a good scene of the shark darting back and forth, trying to get past me. But it was trapped, so it turned around and shot into a tight crevasse at the rear of the cave. We checked our pressure gauges and made our ascent to 15 feet where we decompressed before surfacing.

So it had been going. We had worked shark corner for two days, drifting with the current and filming until it was time to move on to the next fabulous location. Once again Tubataha was paying off with some extraordinary diving.

It was seldom that we dived off the *Lady*. Usually we traveled by skiff and outboard to the nearby reefs. Early on in the trip, John, Pam, and I ran about a quarter of a mile slightly north from the southwest corner of the south reef to anchor at the edge of the wall. It was to be one of our first dives together and as we raced along I thought how gratifying it was to have my son with me. He was 26 and, along with his sister Kim, one of my two best friends. And Pam, whom I met on this second trip, was to become my wife a couple of years later.

The sun was well up off the horizon and the water flat and sparkling. Through its transparent surface the reef looked rich with corals. When I dropped into the water and the bubbles cleared, it fairly took my breath away. As in the Red Sea, hundreds of tiny orange and purple jewel-like fish danced in the morning sunlight, obviously delighted with their station in life. And the varieties of corals seemed endless. Great crowns and tables of plate corals abounded among a field of white stinging hydroids. Some corals were distinctly pink, or blue, or green. And, stretching out from the edge that was barely ten feet deep was the deep, rich blue of the open ocean. It was a great place to introduce John and Pam to Tubataha.

We pushed out and drifted down the face of a sheer wall

skimming over a dozen different varieties of leather coral. At 50 feet, clumps of pink, orange, and yellow soft corals either grew on the wall or hung on the tips of whiplike corals. And, I saw more varieties of crinoids here than anywhere else I've dived. They blossomed in violent crimson, pure white, yellow, green, and black.

We were experiencing change of moons from a quarter to a half and at various locations we ran into strong tidal flows and limited visibility. So we worked accordingly, searching for spots along the wall where we could work close, out of the current. For the most part visibility ranged around 80 feet. Some days it would drop to 60 feet, but on others we could easily see 125 feet underwater both vertically and horizontally.

One morning around 6:00AM we woke up to a magnificent sunrise playing on a still sea. Gentle splashing drifted across the water from 100 yards off the bow, breaking the quiet dawn. Manta rays were feeding at the surface. A couple of us slipped into the water and swam into the shallows with our cameras. The water was warm, but numerous tiny stinging things were having a field day on the naked portions of our bodies. The water was also clear, but rich with plankton and this is what attracted the mantas to feed. Since it is close to the equator, the sun rises fast and by the time we spotted the rays we had enough light to shoot by.

There were four mantas sweeping back and forth with their cavernous mouths expanded to flood vast quantities of water through their gills, straining out the life-giving miniature food-stuff. The rays were small, about five to six feet across the wingspread, but they brought back fine memories of their giant kin that I rode on and filmed in the Sea of Cortez. The rays would make a leisurely run past us, feeding and swooping and banking as they approached. At first they seemed shy, but after awhile

A diver photographs a manta ray early one morning close to the Lady of the Sea. *Photo by Jack McKenney.*

they let us get quite close. At times a couple of them practically bumped into my camera, they were so intent on feeding. When they disappeared we'd hang at the surface and two or three minutes later they'd make a return run. We spent an hour with them and soon half a dozen other divers joined us. It was a pleasant way to begin a day of diving.

Not far from the lighthouse on the south reef is the *Delsan,* a rust-riddled shipwreck. She stands high and dry on the reef and is a poignant reminder of how fallible even great steel ships are when exposed to the forces of nature and the absence of proper lighthouse facilities. The *Delsan* isn't a divable wreck and as the Tubataha Reefs drop off so quickly and are so steep, a good wreck for sport diving hasn't yet been located. Dempsey Pagain, Jr., an American archaeologist who has lived in Manila for more than a dozen years, told me about some Ming dynasty pottery that was discovered at Tubataha; and Pir Castaneda, a Filipino writer, told me he discovered a giant anchor and followed its chain down over the drop-off to more than 150 feet without seeing the end of it, nor what might be attached to it.

The year before, when I was producing *Beneath the Sulu Sea* with my former wife Sari, we had traveled to Apo Reef, much farther north in the Mindoro Sea, to dive on and film a wreck there that I had heard about. After we furtively searched for two days, the lighthouse keeper finally put us onto it. She lies off the southeast reef in 35 feet of water and is one of the prettiest wrecks I have ever dived on.

The wreck is remarkably intact and sits upright on a bright sand-and-coral-patch bottom with the bow firmly embedded in the reef. This unnamed wreck appears to have been a fishing vessel. She's about 60 feet long and has a vibrant mantle of some of the most delicate and lovely corals that ever adorned a shipwreck. We spent a late afternoon and half the next day filming and photographing this lovely jewel. It's the type of wreck that every diver dreams of diving on one day. It was so beautiful and pristine that Sari and I almost felt we were trespassing. We took great care while swimming around and through it not to break off any of the corals. A careless flipper could easily demolish some of the big plate corals topping the two upright stanchions at the stern of the ship, or along the railings.

Numerous soft corals adorned the windows and doorway of the tiny wheelhouse. Rubbery, pliable leather corals were splattered along the sides of the vessel and hundreds of tiny fish flitted about the wreck. At night, under the bright intensity of our lights, we discovered flatworms mating in the sand near the stern and I had a field day with my macro camera system. I had never

Sari swimming along the Apo Island wreck. Photo by Jack McKenney.

seen so many tiny crabs and worms and other strange things on a night dive. At times the action was so thick that the flatworms and nudibranchs, just inches in front of my camera lens, were obscured.

It was with happy hearts, but saddened spirits, that we left this little jewel of a wreck. I hope others who are lucky enough to visit it will treat it gently. It would be a shame to see it worn down by diver pressure.

The Philippines is a unique blend of contrasts. Manila is much like any major city with handsome buildings, comfortable hotels, traffic jams, and the hustle and bustle of people who make up such a vibrant metropolis. Yet, half an hour out of the city, farmers still plow their fields with carabao, a type of water buffalo.

A six-hour drive north will deliver you to Banaue, where rice terraces that produce much of the Philippine's rice crops were

Photo by Jack McKenney

hand-carved out of the mountain slopes more than 2,000 years ago. It's like stepping out of a time machine into a very lovely and historical mountainous part of the islands. There's a river called Pagsanjan where boatmen paddle their customers up river in log canoes and forge a series of rapids by literally jumping out and running and hopping from rock to rock to make their way upstream. At the end, everyone can raft under a waterfall to cool off.

The Philippines is a fascinating country. But it's the diving— some of the most beautiful I've ever experienced—that makes it so special. Many of my friends and family who have dived all over the world agree that the Sulu Sea and the Mindoro Sea, where lies the little Japanese fishing wreck, offer some of the finest diving to be found anywhere.

JACK McKENNEY

The Bay of Dolphins

T he water was calm and clear and the sky a bright electric blue with white cotton clouds scudding by in the soft morning breeze. While swimming along I glanced up at the lush green emerald jungle spilling down from the high cliffs to the volcanic black boulders that surrounded the picturesque bay.

Swim fins, mask, and snorkel were my equipment for the day, along with a high speed Milliken 16mm camera. The warm sun felt good on my back as I swam through the cool water toward one of the schools of spinner dolphins. We were on location at Fernando de Noronha, an archipelago about 200 miles off the coast of Brazil not far from the equator. This beautiful group of six main islands and 14 rock outcroppings is known to Brazilians as Emerald of the Atlantic.

In 1502 Portugal laid claim to the islands and over the next 200 years the Portuguese built some 17 forts. One of them— Nossa Senhora dos Revillios—built in 1723 still stands very much intact. Brazil, although long since independent, has remained a Portuguese-speaking country. And Emerald of the Atlantic is a very apt description for this exquisite group of islands ruggedly thrusting up its craggy mountain peaks and gorgeous sand beaches from beneath a warm, clear blue ocean.

I swam on and suddenly 15 to 20 spinners, huddled together, greeted me curiously as they approached. Two of them were mating and the rest seemingly ran interference for them. The camera was instantly at my eye, recording the scene. And at that moment, about two weeks into the expedition, it suddenly dawned on me, actually hitting me like a ton of bricks, how very important this project was. When they passed, I looked up at the incredibly beautiful and pristine surroundings and realized that what we were doing here could have a profound effect on these wonderful animals.

I am not a fanatic or a bleeding-heart environmentalist, but I do believe there are conservation and environmental issues that everyone should support. I think most people do favor, emotionally, at least, the preservation of species. After all, what's to be gained by not championing their cause? And how much time and effort does it take to really make a difference? If everyone just spent one or two hours a year writing to concerned government officials about a specific problem, you can bet there would be significant action taken. After all, politicians don't like to be inundated with unfavorable mail from their constituents. And how much money does it take to join and support organizations such as the World Wildlife Fund, the Sierra Club, or The Cousteau Society—organizations that really do make a difference?

Someday, this difference is going to be critical: The scientist, Edward O. Wilson, states that by the 1990s we could be losing, from our planet, more than 10,000 species of plants and animals each year, many of them having gone unrecorded. Some of these species would be lost owing to natural attrition, but far too many would disappear because of man's folly and mismanagement. In 10 years that would be 100,000 species. In 20 years—200,000.

Where would we reach the point of no return, the point where all life would be threatened?

Like many people, I've done little but pay lip service to some of the very obvious environmental problems that face us around the world. Like others, I, too, keep busy with day-to-day routines working, raising a family, and paying bills. But on this very special day, that perfect day, when the water was clear and the sky was blue and the dolphins were free and unencumbered, I realized I had to do just a little bit more.

My wife Pam (we got married on one of the storybook beaches on the main island during the trip) and my son John and I were brought down as a film team by Russell Wid Coffin, a Brazilian conservationist, to produce and shoot a film about the archipelago and its wildlife, and more specifically to focus on the vast school of spinner dolphins that were first observed here around 1700 by a French expedition.

As far as anyone knew, no other location in the world has had such a consistently large school of spinner dolphins returning to the same spot for the last few hundred years. Our aim was to produce a film that would help convince the Brazilian government how important it is to set aside part of Fernando de Noronha as a preserve, not only for their own countrymen, but for the benefit of all mankind. The government was seriously considering developing the islands as a major tourist resort.

From conception to realization, such a vast undertaking as establishing a marine preserve, however, takes a tremendous amount of determination, time, dedication, and money. A few key people had put in a lot of effort on this project, but the instigator and driving force behind it was Russell Coffin.

Russell is a young, blond, unpretentious, wealthy business-man who looks more at home riding a surfboard or donning scuba gear than he would wearing a three-piece suit to board meetings. He and his sister, who own five Coca Cola bottling plants just outside Rio, were born in Brazil of American parents. Russell was educated in the States, but his heart and roots are permanently planted in Brazil.

When he first saw Fernando de Noronha and the Bay of Dolphins, Russell immediately recognized the need to have this grand wilderness area set aside as a legacy for future generations before the big commercial interests arrived to develop the main island. Using his own money he formed the *Comite Pro-Parque National Marinho de Fernando de Noronha*, and contracted with me to produce a film.

Guy Pelland, a talented Canadian photographer who had been working on Grand Cayman as a dive guide, is Russell's friend and one of the founding members of the marine park committee. Guy and his wife June made up the rest of the film team. My son John was camera and dive assistant and Pam was production assistant. Edson, Tola, and Antonio made up our boat crew and dive guides.

Russell had started a small diving concession on the main island—with three dive boats—which services up to six or eight divers a week. He established the business to have a base of operations there while devoting his energies to establishing the marine park. The Brazilian military was in charge of the island, governed by an Air Force colonel.

I got to know Russell pretty well in the five weeks we worked together. He has enough money and is good looking enough to hot-rod it around Rio as a wealthy playboy. But he doesn't like to wear or drive his wealth, is married and has a lovely family. When he first sailed to the remote archipelago, he became so concerned about leaving it pristine and unspoiled that he

Fernando de Noronha, a beautiful archipelago about 200 miles off the coast of Brazil. Photo by Jack McKenney.

decided to spend both time and money to see a Fernando de Noronha nature preserve become a reality.

There is a small Spartan hotel on the island that is always full. The food is terrible and the rooms are bleak compared to American standards. But, each week a new batch of 100 tourists flies into the island, and twice a week a majority of them come to the bay in the hotel boat to swim with the dolphins.

The Bay of Dolphins is right out of a storybook setting. Each day as our vessel, the *Thor*, would enter the tiny bay, spinners would rush in from all sides to ride our bow wave. We could easily count 20 of them racing along, while other groups snorted and leaped from the water, sometimes spinning as many as three or four times before falling back into the glistening water.

We'd anchor to a permanent buoy that was established for the few boats that do come into the bay so the dolphins aren't dodging anchors raining down from above. When we entered the water we'd have to swim for 100 yards before we first glimpsed them.

Unlike bottlenose dolphins, the stars of sea aquariums and marine-land shows around the world, spinners don't do well in captivity. In a short period of time they become morose and depressed, refusing to eat, so they have to be released. Consequently, they have been studied very little while in captivity and not at all in the wild.

The spinners seemed to live a pretty regular existence. Each morning they would return early to the bay to socialize and mate after feeding at night in the open ocean. On almost every dive we observed dolphins mating, but most of the time when we approached, other dolphins would swim in front of us, as if to give the amorous pair some privacy. And it was the same with baby dolphins; the adults were very protective when we approached too close.

Some of the dolphins had perfect circular indentations on their flanks about the size of a silver dollar. Guy explained they were probably caused by the cookie cutter shark. The cookie cutter is a deep-water shark that rises toward the surface at night

Spinner dolphins underwater, heading right at the author. Photo by Jack McKenney.

to feed. When the dolphins are feeding, the sharks, which average only a foot in length, dart in, grasp the dolphins and spin around. The knifelike edge of the lower teeth carves out a perfect round plug. Usually, the dolphins survive the small incision, but it does leave a nasty scar.

The spinners would leap from the water, spinning in mid air and then often repeat the jump again until they would fall back physically spent. At least it appeared they were tiring because the jumps would get shorter and shorter. It isn't known exactly why they do this, but it's assumed it has something to do with communications.

In the early morning hours the dolphins were generally playful and curious. After they approached, speedily swimming

A snorkler swims down toward three dolphins. Photo by Jack McKenney.

circles around us, they darted away quickly, only to return a few minutes later. If we swam toward the bottom, the dolphins would also descend. But after an hour or so their curiosity waned and we had to swim a little harder to stay up with them.

The previous year Russell and Guy attempted to use scuba in the bay and found that the bubble noise irritated them. Another time, when Russell used a Tekna diver vehicle just outside the bay, the noise attracted some of the spinners and they swam with him for about 10 minutes.

Based on these two incidents we decided to conduct some experiments. When we tried scuba gear in the bay the dolphins shied away and wouldn't come near us. But, when we only used vehicles, and then in conjunction with scuba, the difference was

A sideview of spinner dolphins underwater. Photo by Jack McKenney.

like night and day. At times we had 40 to 50 dolphins zipping along beside us, in front of us and, occasionally, following us.

If we singled out one of the dolphins and chased it, it would lead us down, then quickly shoot up to the surface for air, then in and around some of the other animals. It seemed as though the animals really did enjoy the game of being chased. Also, it was evident that these dolphins enjoyed the motor noise of the vehicles, but not the divers' exhaust bubbles. But, the steady hum of the vehicles seemed to cancel out the exhaust bubbles as far as the dolphins were concerned.

On a dolphin project that I took part in years ago in the Bahamas, music was introduced underwater to spotted dolphins and they loved it. They swam circles around the underwater speaker. We even filmed sound engineer Steve Gagnan underwater with a waterproof keyboard he designed. Intrigued and totally captivated by the music, the spotted dolphins followed Steve around as if he was the Pied Piper.

The dolphins seem to be attracted by the noises of diver propulsion vehicles. Photo by Jack McKenney.

On the first day we lowered the speaker into the water to see what the reaction from the spinners would be, John checked it with one of us in the water—"testing, one, two, three." His voice came through loud and clear, but created instant chaos. Hundreds of dolphins leaped from the water and took off out of the bay. We were dumfounded!

A few days later we tried it again and the results were the same except that this time only 30 to 40 percent of them responded. We guessed they'd come to tolerate it eventually, but initially a human voice was so foreign to them they immediately took flight. When we slowly introduced the music of Kitaro underwater, the dolphins didn't seem to react one way or the other, but they weren't attracted to it like the spotted dolphins in the Bahamas.

In the five weeks that we were on location in Fernando de Noronha we spent a part of almost every day filming the spinners. There were only a couple of times they didn't show up.

We also explored and filmed much of the rest of the island, including 1,000-foot-high Moro do Pico, a tall, mountainous spire that provides a breathtaking view of the entire archipelago. We filmed Lions Beach where green sea turtles nest—one of the few nesting sites in Brazil—and Bird Island represented another important facet of the wilderness archipelago.

We made more than 10 very exciting dives on the wreck of the *Ipiranga*, a Navy ship that ran aground on a pinnacle at the east end of the island and sank in 190 feet of water just three years before. The wreck was one that Russell and Guy had located on the previous trip and we liberated lots of brass goodies off it, including a Colt 45 that John found buried in silt in the ammunition locker. Wreck fever overtook me, too. I got a compass, the nameplate and a marvelous brass plaque that's engraved "*Ipiranga—Independencia ou Morte.*"

Independencia ou morte. It means independence or death—a fitting epitaph for a brave Navy ship but, I also thought, an omen for what could happen to the dolphins if the islands were developed. If a major hotel was constructed right at Dolphin Bay, the pressure of nearly 600 people swimming out daily to frolic with the animals could do irreparable damage to their habitat. We know for a fact that the dolphins have been here for at least the last few hundred years, but more than likely they have frequented these waters, and this bay in particular, for thousands of years.

Dr. Ken Norris suggests dolphins may actually be altruistic. This would explain why shipwrecked sailors have been rescued by dolphins. In Hank Searles *Sounding* he suggests that cetacea have passed lore from one generation to another.

Just how intelligent are dolphins? The brain of a dolphin is about 300 grams larger than man's. Its echolocation system is

John McKenney with a .45 handgun and a line gun that he recovered from the wreck of the Ipiranga. *Photo by Jack McKenney.*

superior to our hearing and sight. Yet man, with his supposedly more developed intellect, has been an abomination and scourge to his own kind and other species throughout history. Between 1960 and 1975 the number of dolphins killed in commercial tuna nets has been estimated at between three and five million. World consciousness has somewhat alleviated the problem, but despite such measures as the Marine Mammal Protection Act passed in 1972, thousands of dolphins continue to be trapped and drowned by fishermen the world over. [In 1990, several large U.S. companies announced they would process only line caught tuna from then on.] In Iki, Japan, the fishermen are paid a bounty for every dolphin they kill.

Years ago I did a magazine shoot of the pupfish that live in Devil's Hole in Death Valley. There are only a few hundred of these tiny, innocuous fish in this one spot in all the world. Developers were trying to build on the surrounding land, but if they tapped into the vast underground water table, the water level would drop and the fish would die. There is a shallow ledge in a few inches of water, which the sun strikes deep in the canyon for a few hours each day. Through photosynthesis the ledge is covered with algae that the pupfish feed on.

At the time, I thought: What does it really matter if a few hundred fish don't survive? The surrounding land could mean homes in a new community and nobody would ever miss the fish. But on that special day in Noronha, it did matter. It mattered that the dolphins would survive and it matters, too, that the pupfish live—simply because they are part of our universe. They're here. They're part of evolution. They're part of the fragile thread that connects all species. There's plenty of other land in the United States for new subdivisions. And there are other locations along the coast of Brazil for tourist development.

Out of film, and swimming back to the boat, I thought: If one day we are truly able to communicate with dolphins, as some scientists suggest, these ancient animals might tell us of their history. If that's the case, it would be a tragic mistake to carelessly allow man's arrogance to continue unabated, to be more concerned about the almighty dollar and hotel profits than we are about a species of animal that might just be more intelligent and more caring than we are.

Epilogue

As this was being written I received a letter from Russell informing me that the Ministry of the Interior had officially taken over jurisdiction of Fernando de Noronha. The new governor is a civilian and pledged his support 100 percent for a marine preserve. Hopefully, by the time this goes to press, the park will be a reality.

JACK McKENNEY

The Stingray Man

S tingrays are among the most common animals seen in tropical waters by divers all over the world. They are related to the shark family and are of the class Chondrichthyes, animals whose bodies are made of cartilage, rather than having a bony skeletal structure. I remember encountering a stingray on my very first dive in the Bahamas back in 1964. Since then I've seen them in every ocean I have dived in, from the Caribbean to the Coral Sea and the Sulu Sea in the Philippines. The prettiest ray I ever saw was a Red Sea variety. It was light brown—almost tan—with bright blue spots on it. Naturally, it was called the blue-spotted ray.

Here in the western hemisphere, one of the more common rays is the southern stingray (*Dasyatis americana*). I've seen them upwards of five feet across at Conception Island in the Bahamas. And it's always intriguing to see their outlines in the sand. They settle down on the bottom and fluff the sand up, letting it fall back over them until they're completely covered except for their eyes and the stinger at the base of the tail. It's their way of hiding, and because they think they are camouflaged by the sand, a diver can practically get right on top of them before they take off.

Two questions often posed by lay people and new divers are: Will the ray attack and is the stinger poisonous? Stingrays do not go out of their way to attack people. Generally, the only time a person is struck by one is if he or she accidentally steps on it, or molests it. The stinger is poisonous, but not deadly. Ben Rose, an instructor and dive guide with whom I worked at the Explorers Club in Freeport, Grand Bahama Island, was struck in the arm by a small ray; he felt feverish and nauseous for a few hours but the next day he was fine and diving again.

As a rule, experienced divers and photographers tend to ignore stingrays because they're not especially photogenic. They're a drab grayish brown in color and don't seem to have much of a personality. It's a lot more fun to photograph curious grouper or flirtatious angelfish. At least that's what I thought until just recently.

I was in Grand Cayman shooting a television segment. We were working with Bob Soto's Diving, which is now owned by Ron Kipp and is one of the oldest diving operations in the Caribbean. It recently celebrated its 30th anniversary. I had heard that Pat Kenney, one of Ron's dive guides, had some pet stingrays over at the north sound and thought it would make a terrific television segment. It sounded intriguing.

Pat is a retired police lieutenant from Wayne, Michigan, who moved down to Grand Cayman more than a decade ago and went to work for Ron. One day, fellow dive guide Jay Ireland, who had stopped at the inside of the fringing reef, noticed a few stingrays underneath the boat. Fishing boats would stop here and throw scraps of bait into the water, which apparently attracted the rays. When Jay discovered them, he noticed they weren't at all frightened and even appeared friendly, so he started to feed them. He told Pat, who was running a couple of diving trips each week to the north shore, so Pat began feeding them on a regular basis. Soon he had as many as 10 rays literally eating out of his hands.

When I jumped into the water for the first time with Pat, I

Off the Carribean island of Grand Cayman a certain group of stingrays are accustomed to being handfed by divers. Photo by Jack McKenney.

was absolutely flabbergasted. Three rays swam up to greet him and almost demanded to be fed. Soon, more rays showed up and they were all over him and me! Pat would hold them, pet them, grab their tails, and let the tail and stinger slide right through his hands. He'd even feed them by holding food in his mouth. It was incredible!

Well, I thought, so much for a lack of personality. Hooray, Jayray and Stubby were regulars. Sometimes a new ray would show up and join in the picnic. Once, a ray that had been hooked by a fisherman and still had the hook in its mouth swam up to Pat's face to show him the hook. Pat attempted to remove it, but had to go back to the boat for a pair of pliers. When he got back down to the bottom, the ray swam up to his face again and turned its underside toward him, as if asking him to remove it. Pat

After the anchor is dropped, the rays appear and surround the divers. As many as 10 have appeared at a time. Photo by Jack McKenney.

extricated the hook and the ray was able to eat again. Now, I know that sounds like an old fisherman's tale, but I had good reason to believe Pat when he told me that story.

In 1981, when the giant manta rays were at El Bajo in the Sea of Cortez, Dr. Ted Rulison and I had removed two 30-inch remoras (suckerfish) from one of the mantas. We stuck knives into the parasitic fish and twisted and pulled with all our strength. They were nasty, tenacious creatures and it took us a good 10 to 15 minutes before we were able to remove them. The manta ray is a wild animal, of course, and could easily have dislodged us with a flip of its giant wings, but it swam around slowly, almost remaining motionless, until we got rid of the remoras. When I had eliminated the first one, the manta swam out a few feet, turned around, and came right back to me, as if expecting me to remove the other one. I then filmed Dr. Rulison killing the remaining one. It made an incredible film sequence. We were totally convinced the giant ray knew we were trying to help it. And, I'm convinced that the smaller southern stingray knew Pat could help it, too.

One scene I filmed of Pat one day happened when two other boats got to the site ahead of us. Pat felt it would be difficult to attract the rays if the other divers were feeding them, but I urged him to give it a shot. We anchored some way off, entered the water, and started swimming over to the spot where Pat usually works with them. I was behind Pat and when I saw a ray approach him from the side I began to film. The stingray acted like a puppy dog trailing behind its master. Pat didn't know it was there—it was up and down, twisting and scampering from side to side, back to me, then off to catch Pat. All I could hear in my mind at the time was light-hearted, scampering, puppy dog music. When Pat stopped, the happy ray swam up from behind and

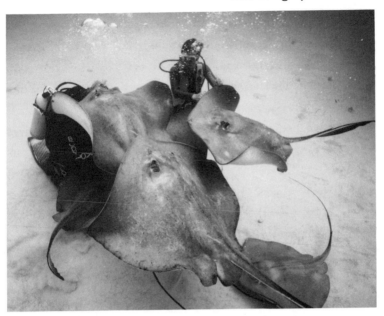

*The rays suck the divers' heads, arms, and hands, looking for food. Photo
by Jack McKenney.*

sucked on his head. It scared the dickens out of him. Soon six
more rays joined us and I got some of the best footage of the trip
that day.

Sometimes the rays suck your head and arms and hands.
They don't really hurt, but if you don't wear a wetsuit, or have a
lot of hair, you might end up with big hickeys all over your body.
One sucked my hand into its mouth and it scared me more than
hurt. Their bony mouths could hurt if they got a good grip on
fingers, but all they want is to eat the fish and squid that Pat brings
down to them.

My wife Pam joined us in the water to feed and pet the rays.
We all agreed it was one of the most fascinating things we've
done underwater and the resulting footage produced an interesting film. The ray's skin is rough, similar to a shark's. And,

when you hold a ray with its underside toward you, its mouth and two gill slits take on the appearance of a weird humanlike face. As a matter of fact, one heavy metal kid that I saw down on Hollywood Boulevard the other day looked very much like one of Pat's stingrays. . . .

JACK McKENNEY

At Work With Cousteau

Nineteen seventy four: That's when I first met Captain Cousteau in his offices on Santa Monica Boulevard in Los Angeles. The Cousteau Society had just been formed and Hillary Hauser and I went over from *Skin Diver Magazine* to interview him. He greeted us cordially, accompanied by his late son Philippe and Norman Solomon, treasurer of the society.

Hillary conducted the interview and I shot pictures. The session began with the customary formal questions and answers, but soon developed into a rapid-fire conversation between him and Hillary. The captain openly revealed his thoughts about a number of subjects and didn't pull any punches. He was quite opinionated and had some definitive, obviously knowledgeable ideas about what was wrong with planet earth, and what role the society could play in making man aware of some of the problems.

As I took picture after picture of spontaneous portraits, trying to catch his deeply lined, hawklike face at its most interesting moments, I was fascinated by his energy and, like every other diver in America, wondered what it would be like to work with him.

Twelve years later I found out. A few days before Christmas, Mose Richards in the New York office called to see if I'd be

Jacques-Yves Cousteau during the author's first meeting with him in 1974.
Photo by Jack McKenney.

available to shoot film with the captain and his son Jean-Michel
in the Falkland Islands, off the tip of South America. Jean-
Michel and I had appeared together at various film festivals and
a few months before I had spoken with him about working
freelance for the society as a cameraman. Even though it would
be over New Year's I said, "Of course!" So, on December 27 I left
Los Angeles to connect with Captain Cousteau in Miami for the
15-hour flight to Puenta Arenas, Chile, with stops in Buenos
Aires and Santiago.

Traveling with the captain is like traveling with the Pope, or the President. He's instantly recognizable and people swarm to him as though he was a Hollywood celebrity. For getting through customs and immigration the recognition is definitely an asset, but after awhile I felt a little sorry for him. People assume it's their right to approach him and even interrupt him when he's talking with someone or conducting business. Lack of privacy is a big price to pay for fame. I was amazed at how gracious he could be, even though in private he complained about it. In Santiago we managed to eventually give the autograph seekers the slip and made it to the Pan Am lounge.

I spent about two hours alone with him and was impressed by two things: his energy (it was still very evident—12 years later) and his sense of humor. We talked about Castro and religion, politics, Haiti, film production, some of his future projects, and the state of the art of video.

I learned a lot from him. And in one lighthearted moment he said, "You know, Jack, in four years maybe I'll write a book on how to dive to 80 meters at 80 years of age, or perhaps *Captain Cousteau's Diet Plan*." (With his lean build a diet book would probably make him $1 million.) I found out, too, that his favorite author is Dr. Seuss.

At 76 years of age, Captain Cousteau was a remarkable, vibrant man. And so far, his life has literally read like the dozens of books he has authored, or co-authored with other notables in the diving and literary field.

In 1943, with Emile Gagnan, he co-invented the Aqua-Lung demand regulator, providing a passport to the underwater world for literally millions of people. Over the next four decades he conducted scientific expeditions in just about every major body of water on planet earth.

In 1950 he acquired and outfitted *Calypso*. He was responsible for constructing the first self-contained 35mm underwater camera, also named "Calypso," forerunner to the Nikonos. His diving saucers have carried scientists and cameramen into the deeper realms of the sea. His highly successful Conshelf experiments concluded with six men actually living underwater for 27 days at depths to 120 meters. He produced nearly 80 films, winning Oscars and Emmys along the way. And on May 23, 1985, at a White House ceremony, President Reagan presented the captain with the Presidential Medal of Freedom.

But perhaps his most important legacy is making us aware, regardless of political boundaries, how important all aspects of the environment are—especially the oceans, which make up three-quarters of this planet. Little wonder then that this man, who has given so much to his fellow men, is so revered.

To get to the Falkland Islands from Santiago, Chile, we first flew to Puenta Arenas where we stayed overnight. I was amazed at how bright it was at 10:00PM. It didn't get dark until midnight. The next morning we boarded an eight-seater Cessna and flew through some breathtakingly beautiful glacier passes. Here, in Tierra del Fuego, at the bottom of the world, the air was so crisp and clear that it almost crackled and the heavy slate-gray clouds provided an awesome contrast to the white, snow-capped Andes.

On board were the captain, biologist Dr. Francois Serano, Leslie High, Gonzolo Campos, myself, and a young Argentinean pilot with whom the captain had previously flown. Francois had joined up with us in Santiago as the expedition scientist. He worked full time for the Cousteau Society. Gonzolo, a young Chilean student from Puenta Arenas studying for his PhD, was a guest, invited at the last moment. Leslie was the Cousteau liaison for the expedition.

(Later on, a few days out to sea, we learned our young pilot and six Americans were killed when the same Cessna got caught in a snowstorm in the mountains and crashed. It happened over New Year's.)

An hour and a half later we landed in Puerto Williams, Argentina, where we were greeted by the crew and settled in on the *Alcyone*, Cousteau's new windship. After clearing customs in Ushuaia, Chile, we began our journey out of the Strait of Magellan, which separates South America from Tierra del Fuego, and sailed east across 350 miles of South Atlantic ocean. It took two days of sailing to arrive at Port Stanley, capital of the Falkland Islands.

Alcyone, was the second daughter of Aeolus, Greek god of the wind, and is an appropriate name for Cousteau's new sailing ship. The vessel is 103 feet long, 29 feet wide and operates on the same principle as a conventional sailing ship, yet with greater efficiency achieved by combining hydrodynamics with aerodynamics. Its two metal turbosails are 33 feet 5 inches high, providing a surface area of 226 square feet

An airplane is lifted through a decrease in air pressure above its wings and an increase in air pressure below them. Basically, the turbosails work the same way, except in a vertical mode rather than a horizontal one. A shipboard computer and diesels work in conjunction with the turbosails to provide the greatest possible efficiency. Thirty-five percent is saved in fuel costs.

Alcyone is really a prototype of what will possibly be the accepted way to travel on the sea in the future. But, as a major expedition vessel, unlike the *Calypso*, it is just too small to operate from comfortably.

My role was to shoot film both topside and underwater. There was no camera room and I didn't have an assistant, so I

Alcyone in one of the picturesque harbors in the Falkland Islands. Photo by Jack McKenney.

was relegated to changing film and maintaining all the cameras in my cramped bunkroom, which I shared with Gonzolo. There were two bunks, a small closet, and a tiny desk.

Fortunately for me, most of the crew spoke English. Clay Wilcox, a strapping 19-year-old American, was on board as a diver and cook. Clay had been with the Cousteaus a little more than a year, was learning French as he was going along and becoming very proficient at it. During meal times most of the conversations were conducted entirely in French, unless there was something they wanted me to know. Otherwise it was strictly French. I didn't mind because I was so preoccupied with the responsibility of filming that I welcomed the time to tune out and think about the best ways to create "little stories," as the captain called them, out of any subject matter we filmed.

The main thrust of the expedition was to dive and explore

Cape Horn and the Falkland Islands and document anything and everything of interest. I had commitments back in the States, so I agreed to stay on only for the Falkland Islands portion of the filming.

Port Stanley is a picturesque little community of Scottish descent with a population of around 900. It was here in April of 1982 that Argentina went to war with Britain over the Falklands (the Argentineans call the islands Malvinas). The scattered remnants of war debris can still be found on the outskirts of town. Another 900 or so people live scattered on small farms on some of the other 100 islands.

The islands are barren and bleak and it rains 250 days out of the year. Temperatures range from 36 to 49°F in the summer. Sometimes there are days of very warm sunshine in late December and January. We hit it lucky. Much of the time it was sunny and pleasant; but some days it was blustery, rainy, and cold, and if that was typical (it is) I couldn't imagine wanting to live here.

Diving was cold, but fascinating. Dominique Sumian, the big burly lead diver who had been with the Cousteaus for almost 20 years, Bertrand Sion, the alternate cook and diver, Francois, and I loaded up an inflatable boat with our dive gear, a generator, lights, and two cameras. Ange Legall ran the boat for us and in half an hour we were anchored over the wreck of an old clipper ship.

Water visibility was about 40 feet. Thick kelp covered the bottom and spread out profusely over the surface. Dragging the light cable through it was strenuous. Most of the Cousteau underwater footage is filmed from the subjective viewpoint, with the divers who handle the lights often appearing in the film. Bertrand, who was the light man, was a strong diver, so from that standpoint it made things a little easier for me.

The water was icy cold so it was strictly drysuit diving.

Pushing a camera around while wearing a bulky drysuit in thick kelp can be pretty tiring, but the diving was pretty and we were able to get some interesting footage. There was a remarkable scarcity of fish, so I assumed this is why the Falkland Islanders choose to eat mutton almost every day. There is no fishing industry to speak of.

As we swam over the wreck, discovering a number of brass portholes and a large boiler, I thought it must have been an absolute nightmare for the sailors on board when she ran onto the reef in these freezing cold waters. Chances of survival had to be practically non-existent.

One fascinating aspect of the diving is that the kelp beds, very similar to those off California, were decorated with huge clusters of sponges hanging from the stalks and fronds. Some of the sponges were 15 feet long and bright orange in color when we bathed them with lights.

For topside filming I used an Aaton, one of the finest cameras available for serious 16mm work. The underwater cameras are the same basic design the Cousteau team has used for years. They are a tube design with noisy, but rugged, Bell and Howell movements. Instead of a co-axial (side-by-side) film load like the Aaton, the underwater cameras feature in-line camera spools. Not only do the subsea cameras not have reflex viewing, but they don't even have viewfinders. The captain says the best practice for filming underwater is to be proficient at shooting skeet. "It should be an instinctive reflex action," he says. "It's like shooting from the hip." And, as long as you know what field of view each camera covers, it works well. The two primary cameras use a 5.7mm lens and a 9mm lens. A third camera has a 16mm lens for close-ups.

For the "Rediscovery of the World" program, the Cousteau

team developed some interesting new diving gear. Inside the silver backpacks are four high-pressure cylinders containing 140 cubic feet of air at 5,000 psi. The divers don't use pressure gauges, but have a unique reserve system. When it gets difficult to breathe, a valve is turned, equalizing a tank of air into all four cylinders. The dive continues, and when it's necessary to equalize the air again, an ascent is made. The units are very light and comfortable to wear.

One day when it was drizzling, overcast, and windy, Francois, Clay, Ange, and I ran by inflatable for about 45 minutes to a headland outside the harbor to film dolphins that had been spotted earlier on a recon dive. We brought Tekna diver vehicles with us that we would use if we were fortunate enough to find the animals. Frankly, I had my doubts we'd be so lucky. But as soon as we got to the spot we saw them.

Water visibility was poor—only 10 to 15 feet. We dropped to the sandy bottom and Clay and Francois started buzzing around me with the vehicles. Soon the dolphins joined them. They were large black and white animals distinctively marked and full bodied. For 20 minutes they zoomed in and out of camera range, suddenly appearing out of the haze and quickly disappearing, then zooming in again. But with the wide-angle lens, I was able to get some good footage even under those poor conditions. I wasn't able to tell for sure, but the animals were possibly either the rare Peale's dolphin or the hourglass dolphin, both indigenous to the waters off southern South America.

The ride back was bouncy and against the icy, spray-slinging wind. I glanced at Clay and Francois from my perch at the bow of the boat. They were cringing from the cold while I was trying to keep my hands from freezing while holding onto the camera. We were cramped and uncomfortable and wanted to be back aboard *Alcyone*, but we wouldn't have traded the experience for anything—especially Francois. I've never seen anyone get so excited about what he saw and discovered underwater. However, I suspected that Ange, who was running the inflatable, would much rather have stayed back on board ship.

About halfway into the expedition Jean-Michel joined us and we sailed for Bueschene Island, 12 hours out of Port Stanley. Up to now we had been diving around the town and making excursions to some of the closer islands. If you look at a map of the Falklands, Bueschene sort of hangs way off to the side by itself. It is very remote and cut off from all semblance of civilization. There isn't even a lighthouse on the island. Most of the time weather is totally inhospitable, but our luck held and for three days we at least had sunny, if very windy, afternoons. As it proved, working on Bueschene was one of the most incredible experiences of my life.

The island, which is a nature preserve, is roughly two miles long and half a mile wide. And it is literally covered with birds. It is enveloped with a throng of birds so vast, that to gaze upon the sight from the highest part of the island makes you gasp in wonder. Surely, there are only a handful of people in this world who have ever set foot on Bueschene and not too many more who have even heard of it—but I was one of them. And, as I gazed out over the squawking, tightly packed mass of feathered creatures, I thought how fortunate I was to experience this!

Aerial surveys have established that the following bird population lives on Bueschene:

Rock hopper penguins—300,00 couples
Albatross—170,000 couples
King cormorants—5,000 couples
Gentu penguins—3,000 couples

Bueschene Island, a nature preserve about two miles long and one-half mile wide, is literally covered with birds. Photo by Jack McKenney.

That's almost a million birds! Probably more than that since the survey was made. (And you're right, there's a lot of bird poop there.) In addition, there are other species of smaller birds on the island, including the caracara. They are a handsome hawklike bird, resembling vultures, and feed on carrion.

Jean-Michel, Francois, Michel Treboz (the sound man), and I set up individual coffin tents on the island to spend the first night ashore. As we were trying to secure tent pegs in the rocky ground, I said to Jean-Michel, "You know, I really hate camping." He laughed, and said, "I do, too. . . ."

From the start we fell in love with the tiny and inquisitive rock hopper penguins. They marched through our camp as though they owned the place (which they did), and pecking at the tent ropes and anything else that caught their attention. Later, when I was off by myself filming them, I would set the camera down and shoot from ground level. If I was really still, they'd come within inches of me and peer into the camera lens. They were incredibly trusting and inquisitive. And why not? Man is not their natural enemy, probably nothing more than a curiosity to them.

It was amazing to watch them march up and down from the high ground, scampering over the rocks to get back and forth to the sea. In the course of a day, they put in a lot of hiking time getting to their feeding grounds.

Covering a small part of the island was six-to-eight-foot high tussock grass, which served as sanctuary and burrowing grounds for a few of the penguins, as well as nesting sites for some of the caracara. On more than one occasion, when we walked too close to their nests, these birds would attack us from behind. One drew blood when it actually grabbed Jean-Michel's head. Fortunately, Jean-Michel has a thick head of hair, or it could have been pretty painful.

The albatross built round, flat-topped, mud nests and on most of the nests were fuzzy babies, all seemingly yelping together. It was possible to sit right in front of them just a foot or two away and frame the camera for some remarkable close-ups. But, when they got excited they often had the bad habit of regurgitating a foul-smelling, pink, oily liquid. On one occasion I was sitting in front of a nest with my leg stretched out to the side when all of a sudden, the baby bird up-chucked all over me. Fortunately I was wearing heavy duty slickers, but the stink and the stain seemed to be permanent.

On one occasion I put my hand out to see how close I could get to another baby albatross and promptly had my hand covered in bird vomit. And, when I let the camera tilt back on the tripod while I cleaned it off, an overhead shooter let fly and hit the camera lens smack in the middle. I guess I was lucky though, for having spent three days with a million birds on a half-mile by two-mile island that was all that happened.

While we were working on shore, Dominique took the captain completely around the island by inflatable, exploring anything that looked interesting. They discovered a tunnel that went back into the island for about 200 yards. It opened into a small amphitheater about 100 yards in diameter. At the end was a pool filled with all sorts of interesting things.

Later, Ange took Bertrand, Francois, and me back in and we made a couple of dives. There was an incredible storm of dazzling and ethereal planktonic travelers in the basin made up of ctenophores, jellyfish, salp, and a few tiny fish. Francois was absolutely beside himself, especially when he discovered what appeared to be a new species of squid. The little guy was no larger than the tip of my thumb and partially transparent. We surfaced with Francois holding the prize in his cupped, bare hands (he never wore gloves when we were diving even though the water temperature was around 45°F). Excitedly, he exclaimed to no one in particular. "Look at zis little squid, all alone in za world."

I'm sure there must have been a few more around, but we didn't find any and it wasn't in any of the textbooks we had on board the *Alcyone*.

The three days we spent on the island were exhausting! On the day Francois discovered his squid, I had shot ten magazines of film, and three of those were underwater. I had traipsed from one end of the island to the other carrying the camera, extra lenses, tripod, and two spare magazines with me. When I exposed all of the film, I'd have to walk back and reload. Usually, if a wildlife cameraman shoots six rolls of film in one day, he's doing well; but when he has to be his own assistant, do all of the film loading and diving, too—it was a tired Jack McKenney who dropped into his bunk that night. But, I'd do it again in a minute. Bueschene, both topside and underwater, remains one of the most fascinating and interesting locations I have ever visited!

So, 12 years after meeting Captain Cousteau, I found out what it was like to work with him. Early, I caught on very quickly that I had to be prepared for almost anything at all times. He often changed his mind with little or no warning and you were expected to be ready to change shooting tactics immediately. One morning he dragged me out of bed at 5:30AM to film a school of birds diving in the water about 100 yards away. It was overcast and raining, but he wanted it filmed. As a matter of fact, he was extremely enthusiastic about it. And, even though it ended up on the cutting room floor, as I expected it would, he was right in wanting it covered. When shooting documentaries, you have to be ready at all times to take advantage of whatever comes along. Generally, you don't get a second chance. One day, though, I did.

While we were in Port Stanley we awoke one morning to find that a seal had climbed into our inflatable for a snooze. We shot a nice little sequence of the captain discovering it, and shooting pictures of it. Gradually the rest of the crew became involved until, without warning, the seal abruptly slipped over the side and disappeared. I felt the sequence was incomplete without getting a shot of it leaving and felt pretty discouraged about it. But the following morning it returned, so I set up the camera and filmed while someone shooed it into the water. I got my shot, so the sequence ended up complete and appears in the film *Waters of the Wind*.

Captain Cousteau is a sailor at heart, and loves to be on the bridge of his ship. He admits that it's not a way of life for everyone. "It's a hard life," he said, "especially being away from

Captain Cousteau at the helm of Alcyone *with Michael Treboz. Photo by Jack McKenney.*

home and loved ones for such long periods of time." He's been at sea for more than 50 years. And his story is certainly an incredible one. I've respected and admired the man ever since I began diving, but having worked with him, my admiration and respect went up a hundredfold.

Yes, it is a difficult life, but full of discovery and excitement, wonder, and adventure! It was nice to get home, to sleep in a king-sized bed, to see my kids and Pam, who was later to become my wife; and to eat pizza and go to a movie. But often, when I'm sitting at my desk working, I glance up at the wall at the picture of Captain Cousteau that graces the booklet of his "first 75 years" celebration. He inscribed it for me, and it reads:

> Jack! Your company on board *Alcyone* in the Falkland Islands was a lot of work—well done—but also a pleasure for all of us! Come again!
>
> J. Y. Cousteau

I think back, and remember, not the icy cold water we had to dive in, or the exhaustion after a hard day's work. I can't feel the stinging cuts I had on my hands, or the numerous bumps on my head for not ducking in the low-ceilinged ship. And I forgot about the diarrhea that affected most of us for part of the trip. Instead, I remember the captain sharing good humor (in French) at the dinner table with his crew who obviously liked and respected him. I think of the comical rock hopper penguins on Bueschene Island, the majestic emperor penguins on Seal Island, the kelp beds adorned with great clusters of orange sponges and the tiny iridescent and gelatinous space travelers in the underwater amphitheater. I think of the Cousteau mystique, of the good this man and the society have done, and I feel very glad, and just a little smug, that I was a very tiny part of it.

Epilogue

The smugness disappears when I remember the day I spent in Santiago on my way home. I had the full day to see the sights, so I wandered downtown, proudly wearing my *Alcyone* t-shirt. There seemed to be a million people on the streets. I felt something moist lightly hit my back, but thought nothing of it when I looked up and didn't see anything. There wasn't a cloud in the sky. I wandered around the city for a couple of hours, stopped for lunch, got a haircut, and did some shopping. When I got back to my room and took my shirt off I discovered a pigeon had used me for target practice. I wonder if pigeons are related to albatross. . . .

STANTON A. WATERMAN

A true scuba pioneer, underwater filmmaker, lecturer, storyteller, Stan Waterman once aspired to be nothing more than a blueberry farmer in Maine. Luckily for us, this Dartmouth graduate discovered diving and wholeheartedly embraced underwater cinematography. Stan has made more than 22 films, earning three Emmys in the process. His movies delight scuba film festival audiences worldwide. His work has also appeared in seven feature movies, including *Blue Water, White Death* and *The Deep*, and is frequently seen on television.

Dangerous Dudley
Does Cayman

Thei customs inspector surveyed the 17 cases of equipment and diving duffles with a baleful eye. The temptation to crush the mortal traveler with a bureaucratic broadside is always there. Fortunately for this weary traveler, carrying with him the massive encumbrance of equipment for a film production in the Cayman Islands, the inspector was also weary and I was the last in line.

Conspicuous among the aluminum and fiber cases was a large, coffin-size cardboard box. "What's in that?" he demanded. The voice was both suspicious and curious. "Movie props," I answered. He hesitated, then, deciding that postponement of the finish to his day's work wasn't worth indulging in the law's delay, he passed the whole works. Thus did Dangerous Dudley enter Grand Cayman.

Dangerous Dudley is, in fact, the mortal remains of an unnamed Indian, probably a lady, at that; but we'll call her/him Dudley. And, why should I be carrying about a full human skeleton in my luggage? The quest for humor in a film is the answer. In this case it was to be very black humor.

Some months earlier I had shot a film with the Benchley

family for a Cayman dive resort. This film was for Cayman Airways. The idea for Dudley had germinated during the making of the Benchley film. In the harbor at George Town there is a much-dived-upon wreck called the *Balboa*. It's safe to say that almost everyone who dives Grand Cayman dives the *Balboa*. That means about 10,000 people explore the well-worn wreckage each year and perhaps 1,000 of these feed the fish on the wreck. Sergeant majors and yellowtails are the banqueters. Through much experience they have learned to sense even the slightest nuance of the dinner bell. They are faster on the draw than Pavlov's dog. Just start to reach for a plastic bag of food hidden in your BC and you are instantly surrounded, totally enveloped, by fish. Enter the water with a plastic bag visible in your hand and you will descend to the wreck in a cloud of fish. When feeding commences the host divers vanish from sight until the food is gone. I watched Peter and his son, Clayton, experience this alarming phenomenon and from watching what appeared to be a mass of piranhas in a feeding frenzy grew the idea for staging a disaster farce. When the bloated fish dispersed, all that would remain of the diver would be a bleached skeleton.

For awhile the scheme remained nothing more than a figment of my warped humor for the simple reason that I had no skeleton and didn't have a clue of how to come by one. Then a tennis partner who deals in medical publications gave me the number of a medical supply company in Virginia that handles skeletons. I was instructed to ask for Irma. Sure enough, Irma did, indeed, have charge of skeleton sales. In a businesslike voice, untouched by the spirits that had fled those mortal remains, she explained I could have a real human skeleton for $415 or a plastic one for $490. I was, of course, shocked by this evidence of the sad decline of human value in a plastic world. On asking why the

The script called for Lisa to be ravaged by the food-maddened sergeant majors and yellowtails. Photo by Stan Waterman.

difference in price, Irma explained that India had entered the skeleton market some years back and shipped over the real thing at a price that undersold the once popular plastic models. Obviously, our skeleton makers share the same decline that assails the steel makers of this country. To my shame I opted for the cheaper foreign import. A week later UPS delivered to my door the same box that later slipped undetected through Cayman customs.

The scene on the *Balboa* was a huge success. My model, Lisa Truitt, the lovely Our World-Underwater scholarship runner up,

Photo by Paul Humann

was "ravaged" by the food-maddened sergeant majors and yellowtails. When she vanished in their mass I stopped the camera. Paul Humann, an underwater photographer and writer, draped Dudley over part of the wreckage. We dressed our bony prop in Lisa's BC, backpack and tank, fins, gloves, and facemask, stuffed the rib cage with food, stood back and filmed again. Marjorie Lloyd, wife of the governor and an avid diver, was on location, witnessing this horror along with Paul Humann and Barbara Currie. I did cutaways of faces reflecting repugnance, horror, and alarm with all three.

As if this wasn't enough, a sequel to these macabre antics was filmed in the photo lab at a dive resort. A Human Underwater Biology medical tour, led by Bruce and Anita Bassett, got into the act. Fourteen doctors performed dramatic surgery on the skeleton, using divers' knives. Through the magic of not-so-trick-photography they restored the carcass to the living Lisa.

The fun that audiences may have watching these perils and pratfalls is only exceeded by the fun we had producing them. The laughter and pleasure felt by all who participated is a rare and wonderful thing in any business. Fortunately for those of us who make films primarily for diving audiences, humor has always proven hugely successful.

Short of national television, the largest forum for those of us who make underwater films is the growing film festival market. We generally attend these festivals personally. Since one of the few ways an audience can communicate its response to a film is through laughter, we have found, increasingly, that devices like Dudley are well worth the expense and the effort in a film production.

Right now Dudley is resting in my attic, drying off from the Cayman adventure and preparing for a big night next Halloween. However, before we go diving again in another film I suppose I had better think about having him certified. One can't be too careful.

And lest we overdo a good thing I would recall the words of Andre Maurois: "To be witty is not enough. One must possess sufficient wit to avoid having too much of it."

STEPHEN FRINK

Stephen Frink says he "developed an interest in underwater photography en route to a Master's degree in psychology." Although he has had numerous articles published, most of them concern travel or underwater photography. Only rarely does he have the time to work on a story such as the one that follows. He is the world's most frequently published underwater photographer; his credits include most dive publications and many other major magazines.

When not traveling, Frink makes his home in Key Largo, Florida, where he owns an underwater photographic facility. He is also co-owner of a stock photography agency, the WaterHouse. Frink is the author of a textbook, *The Nikonos*

System, Principles of Underwater Photography, written for Nikon, as well as *Stephen Frink's Underwater Guide to the Florida Keys.*

STEPHEN FRINK

Mola Mola Encounter

I was working in the office that day, making duplicate slides for an audio-visual presentation. Deadlines were near and I knew where I should spend the day. But then Mike White called. Mike is the manager of the Key Largo National Marine Sanctuary and we enjoy slipping away to go diving whenever our schedules permit. That day Mike wondered if I would like to go photograph a *Mola mola*. I was surprised and also more than a little skeptical of our odds of success, but it seemed that one of the sanctuary rangers had spotted an ocean sunfish behind a reefline in the Grecian Rocks area, and said he would try to keep it in sight until we were able to rendezvous with him in a fast boat.

It sounded like a long shot. What were the chances that any pelagic fish would wait around while we gathered up dive gear, loaded our cameras, prepared the boat, and headed out to sea? However, I knew the odds of me ever finding a *Mola mola* to photograph in the wild were even less. So, in 30 minutes we were at the dock and in radio contact with the ranger. In 50 minutes we were on location with the *Mola mola* in sight.

I didn't know a lot about the habits of the *Mola mola*. Marty Snyderman had told me they are seen with some regularity in the kelp forests of California, but that they are skittish and difficult

A Mola mola, also called an ocean sunfish, encountered off Key Largo in the Florida keys. The huge fish was about nine feet tall and six feet wide. Photo by Stephen Frink.

to photograph. In the Caribbean I know they are rare, and in the Florida Keys even rarer.

They normally inhabit deep waters, flowing with the current in search of their favorite prey, the purple jellyfish. The fish has massive dorsal and ventral fins, but tiny little tail and pectoral fins. In fact, it appears quite ungainly. Still I had no doubt the fish we were now looking at could swim faster than I, especially since it was about nine feet tall and six feet long.

In order to place the odds of a quick underwater "grab" shot in our favor, Mike and I entered the water ahead of the *Mola mola*—one of us on either side of the fish. The water was murky inside the reefline, and visibility was only about 25 feet so we really couldn't see the fish until we were almost upon it. By chance, and with a diver on either side, the *Mola mola* began swimming in wide circles. I was, fortunately, on the inside of the arc so I did not have to swim as far or as fast to keep up as Mike did on the outside. Still, it took all of my effort to stay within shooting range. I had a Nikonos and 15mm lens, which would have been the perfect tools had the water been clearer, but I found myself wishing for a full-frame fisheye to reduce the water column, because of the turbidity and immensity of the animal. I shot a quick 36 exposures and then climbed aboard the boat to change film.

It seemed we were either wearing out the *Mola mola* or it was no longer threatened by our presence, because when I shot the next roll of film the situation was more controlled. We were still swimming furiously to keep up, but at least we were getting clean head shots of the fish, instead of shooting from the rear. As an afterthought, I took along one of our underwater rental videos, thinking maybe *Mola mola* footage would be good in one of our Key Largo stock videos. However, by then I was tired of trying to keep up with the fish. I shot video film for a minute or so, still swimming furiously.

I saw its eye roll back inside a nictitating membrane when I came too close. I also saw how it siphoned water through its mouth to wash over the gills, and inside the mouth I saw a very strange little shrimp that must have spent its life there in some odd form of symbiosis. When I shoot still photos of my underwater adventures I view the adventure itself on the light table after the fact. But with video my eye is not compressed into a viewfinder and the picture-taking does not intrude on the adventure as it happens. I found the *Mola mola* to be quite wondrous.

Even so, I wanted to shoot more still photographs of this fish,

Ocean sunfish are pelagic animals, generally found only in the deep waters of the open ocean. Photo by Stephen Frink.

perhaps a macro shot of the shrimp inside its mouth. But by then the *Mola mola* was in deeper water, more active than ever and definitely on its way south. I doubt I'll see such a fish in the wild again, and even if I do, I think the chance of getting so near to it is next to zero. But for me this was a special encounter with a special sea animal that took time off from its normal nomadic bluewater life for a visit.

BONNIE J. CARDONE

Born under the sign of Pisces, Bonnie J. Cardone loves water in any form. Her favorite activities (other than scuba, of course) include swimming, skiing, white water river rafting, and ice skating. A diver since 1973, she has authored several hundred articles for *Skin Diver Magazine*, for whom she has been an editor since 1976. Bonnie is also an accomplished photographer and her pictures appear regularly in both *Skin Diver* and other books and periodicals. Her first book, *Southern California Shipwrecks*, co-authored with Patrick Smith, was published by Menasha Ridge Press in 1989.

Shipwrecked!

W hen you travel thousands of miles to go scuba diving you must do so with a spirit of adventure and a good sense of humor. There is no telling whether the trip, the boat/resort, the equipment, the crew/staff, or the food will be exactly as described in the travel brochure or the way someone from another trip remembered them to be. Things change and people's perceptions vary, sometimes drastically. Thus, on a 1984 trip to the Philippines I was mentally prepared to make the best of most situations. I was totally unprepared, however, to be shipwrecked on a deserted island in the South China Sea.

There were 16 of us, all American and all underwater photographers as well as experienced travelers. Our 17 hour flight to Manila and two day stay there to recuperate from it were not extraordinary. We boarded the 102 foot wooden vessel, *Seaquest*, in Batangas and settled in for 10 days of cruising and diving. Four days passed without significant incident.

The diving in the South China Sea was all I had expected and more. Those who had traveled worldwide agreed it was prettier than any other area they had seen. Hard and soft corals were abundant and beautiful. Little fish flitted about everywhere.

There were so many, in so many colors and patterns, it would take years to learn the names of all. Crinoids, a relative of the starfish with feathery looking arms, provided wonderful photographic opportunities. Crinoids come in red, green, yellow, orange and combinations of colors. On two occasions divers saw manta rays. Some were visited by a school of large (75-100 pounds) Napoleon wrasse. I came across a football-shaped animal with bright blue eyes and a body over which washed waves of iridescent colors. We were both startled and the cuttlefish fled before I could take its photo.

We had been on the boat five days when the "experience" occurred. We had been diving Apo for two days. A volcanic island, Apo's center is a brackish lagoon and its white beaches are made of finely crushed coral. The water deepens gradually, reaching about 15-20 feet 100 yards from shore, then dropping steeply to 200 feet. The shallows are filled with hard corals.

I photographed Apo's nonfunctional lighthouse and three apparently abandoned buildings from the boat. The white beaches gave way to brush and trees in the island's center.

We dived the leeside of the island the first day, then went around to the windward side. The second night found us anchored with the bow of the boat in 15 feet of water; the stern and anchor in 200. At nightfall I rushed to the bow to photograph the sun setting behind the island. Someone told me, "Don't bother, Bonnie, there'll be another one tomorrow night." He was wrong.

About 8:30PM I was in my bunk, reading a magazine borrowed from the ship's tiny library. Suddenly the boat hit something and took a slight list to starboard. I went out and looked over the side. We had obviously dragged anchor and been blown aground by the wind. The crew members chattered excitedly in

Filipino. Four of them jumped into the 20 foot skiff and, revving up its outboard, tried to push us off the reef. The wind continued to blow toward the island. The crew then attempted to winch us into deeper water with a stern anchor but that effort also failed.

Most of the 16 passengers got ready to abandon ship. We donned our wetsuits and buoyancy compensators (known as BCs, these are the diver's version of a lifejacket). I put my gloves in my BC pocket, others put booze bottles full of fresh water in theirs. (We didn't know what sort of water supply, if any, the island had.) Our tour leaders, Jim and Cathy, advised us to pack survival kits. Mine was a waterproof box containing my wallet, money, passport, return airplane ticket, lip balm, sunscreen, aspirin, and antihistamines. I put it in a black plastic garbage bag along with my underwater handlight, towel, and sweatshirt, then tied a knot in the top. I also packed all my camera gear and clothing. (Those in the group who neglected to do this regretted it later.)

Once we were all ready to leave the ship we found ourselves with nothing to do. So, we had a party that lasted two hours. Jeff, a member of the crew, entertained us with Dan Fogelberg songs, accompanying himself on his guitar. The dentist from Minneapolis, who had brought his video camera and recorder, filmed the event. We took pictures of each other.

About 10:45PM our divemaster, Abdeen, reappeared after a consultation with *Seaquest's* owner and captain. He told us to relax and take off our wetsuits and BCs. Everything was going to be okay and we need not worry. There would be a high tide at 2:00AM he said, and our boat would float off the reef. With this assurance from a well liked and respected crew member, we gradually drifted off to our cabins and went to bed. We did not question the source of Abdeen's information.

The boat was no longer listing when I fell asleep. It had crushed the coral underneath it and now rocked gently, as if in a cradle.

I was jolted awake at 3:30AM when the boat fell over on its side. I leaped from my bunk and ran outside. It was immediately apparent that someone had misread the tide tables. It was not high tide, it was low tide. We were more solidly aground than ever before and the boat now had a 45 degree list to starboard. Luckily, my cabin was on the port side. When the boat fell over I slid onto the wall. The people on the starboard side, however, had been thrown out of their bunks and nearly out the doors of their cabins. Those who had not packed their photographic equipment had it rained down upon them.

A crew member, sleeping on a bench outside the owner's cabin on the lower deck, had been thrown into the water. While I tried to decide what to do, this man came by and tearfully advised me to go down to the lower deck. I knew this meant we were abandoning ship. I grabbed my survival kit, wetsuit and its assorted accessories, and headed for the stairs at the stern of the boat.

As I reached the dining/social area, the boat lurched a bit more to starboard. I slipped and fell, sliding across the steeply slanting deck into some tables. Someone helped me up. Thoroughly scared, I got downstairs somehow. I was weak-kneed and my arms shook, but I managed to dress in my wetsuit top, booties, and BC. My mask and wetsuit pants must have been dropped when I fell. I didn't think the mask was all that necessary but the wetsuit pants would have been good protection against the coral if we had to swim or wade ashore. I thought about going back upstairs but decided it would be unwise. One member of our group did go back for something. Coming back down he slipped and fell, injuring his back.

Downstairs all was chaotic. Three crew members were in the skiff, but they couldn't agree with those still on the *Seaquest* where to pick up passengers. Most everyone was on the port side, but because of the list that boarding platform was quite high off the water. And, the starboard boarding platform and ladder were underwater. Finally, the skiff came close to the stern. We slipped under the railing there, on the lowest side, and swung ourselves into the little vessel. Before they would accept any men, the crew in the skiff insisted upon getting all the women off the bigger boat. There were only six of us, and we were more than happy to comply. After we were settled, two male passengers and two more crew members were allowed to join us.

Now we had to find a path through the coral to the island in the dark. Great care was needed to avoid damaging the boat and its outboard. After all, we were only the first load, there were still 20 people left on the *Seaquest*. One crew member stood in the bow with my small underwater flashlight, directing the man in the stern who was running the outboard. There was much chattering in Filipino. Finally, we scrambled out of the skiff in calf deep water, about 25 feet from the beach, and waded ashore. This was treacherous going: With each step we sank ankle deep in coral debris. I wore one-eighth-inch thick rubber booties with hard soles, but I could still feel the sharp pieces of coral. Two of the women had no booties and came ashore wearing full foot fins. Some of the men wore shoes. To maintain my balance I dragged my survival kit through the water. It had a large, ragged hole in it when I got to the beach. My towel and sweatshirt were soaked. My waterproof box had not been shut properly and was full of water. My passport, airplane ticket, and wallet were soggy. All of my allergy pills had melted together.

Everyone was ashore but the last group of passengers and crew members when the skiff ran aground. It, too, was abandoned and its passengers forced to walk all 100 yards through the water to safety in the dark.

By 4:20AM we were all on the beach. From it we could see the lights of our boat and hear the gentle roar of its generator. A fire was started and we gathered around. We were chilly, but not cold. The crew members all had on dry, warm clothes; the passengers remained in their wetsuits.

Just before sunup the crew managed to get the skiff off the reef and went to work unloading the boat. I had been using my topside camera to take pictures of the party and had neglected to pack it. It had been on my bunk with the borrowed magazine when I went to sleep. For some reason it and the magazine were in one of the skiff's first loads. As the sun rose over the *Seaquest*, I took my first pictures of it from the beach.

Piece by piece all of our dive and photographic gear came ashore. The cook's propane stove and portable generator were rescued. Food, including a 100 pound bag of rice and three plucked chickens, was salvaged. Cases of beer and soda pop also appeared. The refrigeration on the boat had consisted of blocks of ice. This was gone; water had gotten into the hold and melted it.

We repacked all of our gear under a sun that grew steadily hotter, then, one-by-one trudged off to the abandoned buildings near the lighthouse. To our surprise and delight, breakfast was served about 10:00AM. It was only hardboiled eggs, dry bread, and a warm soda or beer, but it was very welcome. Afterward the crew carried on as if we were still on the boat. The rickety table was cleared off and the porch swept. The china dishes and silverware, salvaged from the boat, were taken down to the beach and washed.

We spent the first day in semi-shock, napping, exploring,

When the tide went out the Seaquest *fell over on her starboard side. Passengers and crew abandoned the ship in the middle of the night. Photo by Bonnie J. Cardone.*

snorkeling, and wondering if this was all a dream and if so, why it seemed so real. I had expected the weather to be hot and muggy. To my surprise, it was more like Southern California in the summer. During the day the temperature would get into the 90s but the humidity was only half what I expected. The nights were cool enough to require a sweatshirt.

Once, when the skiff was not being used to unload the boat, three of us borrowed it for a photographic safari, snapping pictures of the *Seaquest* upon the reef.

Life went on under clear blue skies. All of our men shaved, either using seawater and a safety razor or waiting until dark when the generator was turned on for several hours and using an electric razor. We all also took "Joy baths." The contractor from Virginia had talked about them while we were on the boat and now we all had a chance to try them. They consisted of pouring Joy liquid detergent upon oneself, working up a lather, then rinsing off in the ocean. The contractor claimed you didn't feel sticky or itch afterward. We even washed our hair. The baths were a huge success, but there was only a small bottle of Joy and a lot of people. We hoped the detergent didn't run out before we were rescued.

The lagoon and a small river on the island had brackish water that was not potable. To our great relief, however, there was a cistern next to the buildings that contained fresh water. One of the doctors in our group advised us not to drink it unless it was boiled. Boiling enough water for 35 people on a four burner stove in a hot climate, however, was nearly impossible. We all drank water straight from the cistern and hoped we wouldn't catch anything too nasty.

The island had three structures besides the lighthouse. The cook took over the smallest and it became the kitchen. The second was full of machinery for the nonworking lighthouse. (Later I found out why it didn't work: Pirates had come ashore several months before we got there, stealing what they could and wrecking the rest.) The third and largest structure had five rooms and a sign on the front identifying it as belonging to the Philippine Coast Guard. One of these rooms was dedicated to the Apo Island Marine Reserve. Its contents consisted of litera-ture tacked to the walls pertaining to the reefs around the island. Our island, we discovered, was not deserted, it was inhabited by

From high above Apo Island in the lighthouse, the Seaquest *can be seen lying on her starboard side in the shallows. Photo by Bonnie J. Cardone.*

Rolly, the reserve's "manager" and several incredibly skinny and skittish cats.

Rolly had no running water, no refrigeration, no electricity. I have no idea what he ate other than snails, whose shells I found in the remains of fires. I imagine he also caught fish. Rolly told me he had a wife and children on another island and that he spent three months alone on Apo at a time. He didn't speak English very well but when I asked him how he liked having 35 people living with him, he smiled and told me he was happy to have the company.

The *Seaquest* had a ham radio the owner had used to

communicate with his wife in Manila. He had called her when we decided to abandon ship. The message had been received by another ham operator in Brazil who promised to relay our message to Manila in the morning. The radio was brought to the island and much time was spent devising an antenna for it. Periodically the generator was started and an attempt would be made to reach anyone listening. We had no idea if we were getting out but continued to try.

During the day several fishing bangkas landed in front of what we dubbed the "Apo Reef Hotel." Men would come to the cistern to get water. Abdeen decided to go to Mindoro Island in one of the bangkas. It was about eight feet long and one foot wide. It looked like a canoe with outriggers and was powered by a small diesel engine. It had a propeller that looked no bigger than a pinwheel. Abdeen asked us to autograph his shirt for good luck. We were happy to oblige, feeling he was taking quite a risk. The trip would take several hours.

The *Seasquest's* former passengers settled in the three front rooms of the largest building, the crew members settled in the back two. A hot lunch appeared the first day and supper was served after dark in the light produced by the generator. Both meals featured lots of rice. Somehow the passengers had salvaged their private stores of liquor. At supper, several bottles of wine appeared. Not knowing what the future held, we opened and drank all of them.

After supper, crew member Jeff again entertained us with his guitar. After several glasses of wine everyone sang along with him. In the middle of one song, the boat owner, Toni, yelled for silence. A message was coming over the radio, broken up by static. It was Toni's wife and she was trying to tell us help was on the way. A rescue boat would be arriving at 10:00PM she said. This was several hours away and we were exhausted as well as skeptical. We went to bed.

Most of the vinyl pads from our bunks had been salvaged and the group settled down with boat towels as blankets. Since I was considered a celebrity our host, Rolly, insisted I sleep on one of the four metal cots. There was no mattress for it, just a very thin woven mat. I slept poorly in spite of my exhaustion. When I awoke in the morning I could barely sit up; every bone in my body ached.

The stiffness began to ease as I moved around. The morning was cool and I decided to climb up in the lighthouse and take pictures of our small island and our boat on the reef. I also scanned the horizon for the promised rescue boat and was not surprised when there was none.

When I returned to the Apo Reef Hotel breakfast was being served. There was ham, scrambled eggs, bread, very soft butter and even coffee!

Just after breakfast we saw our first helicopter. It came down low to investigate but didn't land. Rolly said it was an oil company craft. Two hours later another helicopter arrived. This one landed in the middle of the island. It was full of newsmen who interviewed and videotaped us. There was a paramedic aboard and he tried to get our injured man to leave with him. Alan asked if he could take his good friend and personal physician along but was told there was room only for one more passenger. Alan decided to take his chances on the island with the rest of us. The helicopter departed, leaving us no supplies and no idea of what was to become of us.

Just before noon Abdeen returned in the little bangka. He told us the American Embassy, the Philippine government, and Toni's wife all, indeed, knew of our plight. There were no rescue

Passengers and crew on Apo Island watch the skiff arrive, bringing luggage and supplies from the Seaquest. *Photo by Bonnie J. Cardone.*

plans that he knew of, however. Just in case, I packed, leaving one suitcase open to work from.

Just after lunch we heard a plane. I ran out to see what it was. It looked like a fighter jet but stayed high. It circled the island then sped off.

At 2:30PM two fighter jets flew low in front of the Apo Reef Hotel, followed by two helicopters. The supersonic jet noise and the loud whomp-whomp-whomp of the helicopters caused an adrenaline rush. The helicopters hovered over our beach, then landed. When I saw the U.S. Navy insignia on them I felt like cheering and a lump arose in my throat. We *were* going to be rescued!

The door of one of the helicopters opened and the pilot, wearing green coveralls and a helmet, jumped out. When he reached the steps of our hotel, he was given a hearty welcome by Cathy. She literally climbed up him, giving him a bear hug and kiss. She knocked his helmet off in her exuberance.

A conference took place among the pilot, our tour leaders, the boat owner, and our injured man, Alan. The Navy was most anxious to evacuate Alan first and a bit nonplussed to find him walking around and looking a bit stiff but obviously not seriously injured.

I hastily pulled on shorts and a T-shirt over my bathing suit and closed my suitcase. Then I grabbed my topside camera bag and boarded the helicopter. There were ten of us on the first one. The second 'copter took four passengers and a lot of luggage. One of the 'copters refueled and went back for more gear and the last three passengers. The U.S. Marines sent a helicopter but it wasn't needed.

We insisted that Abdeen come with us but the rest of the *Seaquest's* crew and its owner remained on the island. All but six of these, left to guard the boat, were picked up the next day by a Philippine Navy boat.

The helicopters took us to Cubi Point Naval Base. It was wonderful to be off the island and not only be intact but also to have every piece of equipment we started out with. We couldn't thank our rescuers enough. When all of our gear and the last three members of the group arrived, the Navy bused us to Manila. We were celebrities there; we had been front page news for two days. The videotape made by the helicopter newsmen had been shown on TV and viewers given a greatly exaggerated account of our plight. One of the newspapers had first reported our boat sunk and all of us missing. The story had been sent over the AP wire service and we worried our families might have seen it. Several people called home. Mondale and Hart were big news in the States, however, and we hadn't gotten even the briefest of mentions.

From Manila, four of our group elected to return home. The rest of us decided to continue our dive trip. We were bused back to Batangas and spent the next four days at a shore based resort. On our last day there, while diving from two bangkas about 15 minutes from our resort, we saw a small boat coming toward us. Standing next to me, Abdeen remarked, "Here comes the skiff." I didn't comprehend his meaning until the boat drew near and I realized it was *Seaquest's* dinghy, the one that had ferried us to the island in the dark. In it were the last six crew members. They told us they had spent two days and one night traveling from Apo in the open boat. They were going to their homes in a village just minutes from our resort. We exchanged happy greetings and invited them to visit us that night, which they did.

The next day we went back to Manila. We flew to San Francisco via Tokyo and from there, to cities scattered across the U.S. We took with us memories of our trip recorded on film and indelibly engraved on gray matter, as well as a feeling of kinship with our fellow travelers. For all of us a great adventure was over.

BONNIE J. CARDONE

Pinniped Playmates

Their interest was piqued before the boat finished anchoring off San Miguel Island's Point Bennett. Near shore, little heads turned in our direction, letting us know our arrival had been noted. Like a bunch of active children on a school playground, they were ready for any diversion. Right now, we were it. A group of youngsters headed eagerly toward the *Vision*. They swam with their heads out of the water and their huge brown eyes trained anxiously on the boat as if afraid we might weigh anchor and depart without staying to play.

Most of those aboard the *Vision* were members of the Santa Monica Blue Fins dive club. We had chartered the boat for a three day trip to California's northernmost Channel Islands. I had been hoping we would spend at least part of this weekend off Point Bennett, a sea lion rookery. I had been in the water with sea lions before and thought I had finally learned enough to get some good photos. Everyone else went into the water with scuba; two by two the divers disappeared beneath the sea. Sea lions immediately surrounded and followed each buddy team for a while, but quickly grew tired of creatures who paid them no interest.

I had decided to try photographing the sea lions from the

As soon as divers enter the water, they are surrounded by sea lions. Photo by Bonnie J. Cardone.

surface, using snorkeling gear instead of scuba. After all, these are air breathing mammals, spending most of their time in the water at or near the surface. I swam out into the open ocean, about 25 yards off the stern of the boat. The divers who preceded me had been surrounded by sea lions as soon as they jumped in the water and so was I. First the agile animals zoomed in, stopping abruptly five to ten feet away. Then, hanging upside down, they eyed me curiously. Deciding I was harmless, they began circling me, rapidly twisting and turning, leaping and looping. They were so sleek and so fast it was impossible to follow their movements. I hung in the water, with just the tip of my snorkel above the surface, and let them come to me. At least one sea lion delighted in blowing bubbles as it dive bombed me, turning away, it seemed, at the last possible moment.

The youngsters stayed in a group and none of them strayed from it very far for very long. They were constantly in body contact with one another; nose to nose, flipper to flipper or wrestling affectionately.

Sea lions love to zoom right at divers and snorkelers, veering away at the last possible moment before contact. Photo by Bonnie J. Cardone.

Just like little children, however, they had very short attention spans. One minute I was the star attraction, the next I was all alone.

Though wrapped in rubber (a one-eighth inch wetsuit, hood, boots, and gloves) from head to toe, I got cold quickly in the 46°F water. It didn't phase my playmates at all. They seemed impervious to the chill and were obviously enjoying themselves immensely. My fingers were numb by the time I thankfully exposed the last frame of my first roll of film. My fickle friends escorted me back to the boat, but then sped off in search of new entertainment.

Seals, elephant seals and sea lions haulout on the beach at San Miguel Island's Point Bennett. Photo by Bonnie J. Cardone.

The weather was extraordinarily windy that weekend and instead of staying just long enough for one dive, the *Vision* ended up spending all three days at San Miguel. We were at Point Bennett for half a day, long enough for me to shoot three rolls of film and warm up in between.

Although sea lions are found at all the channel islands, they are especially numerous at Santa Barbara and San Miguel. On the latter island a stretch of beach near Point Bennett is a major California sea lion rookery. Stellar sea lions and northern elephant seals haulout and breed here, too. It is the California sea lion juveniles of both sexes, as well as some adult females, that come to play with divers and snorkelers. The males stay on or near shore, patrolling the perimeters of their harems while barking constantly to let potential intruders know they are unwelcome.

We were at Point Bennett the end of May, just before the breeding season (June and July). The juveniles we saw were

Sea lions are incredibly graceful, twirling and twisting as they move through the water. Photo by Bonnie J. Cardone.

nearly a year old. They were very independent, traveling quite a distance from their mothers. According to *Marine Mammals of California*, by Robert T. Orr, California sea lion pups are born between the middle of June and the middle of July. The females begin mating again about two weeks after the pups are born. Although gestation only takes about nine months, through delayed implantation the fertilized egg remains dormant in the uterus for three months. Thus, the pups are born a year apart and mating takes place at the same time each year. While the females stay in one area, the males travel south just before the breeding season, returning to the Northern California coast afterward.

The California sea lion (*Zalophus californianus*) is a member of the order Pinnipedia (meaning fin feet), family Otaridae. There are 31 species of pinnipeds and six are found along the California coast. Four of these belong to the Otaridae family— they are those seals that have ears. In the water, these mammals use their front flippers for propulsion. The males are considerably larger than the females. They have very distinctive heads, quite different from those of the young and the females. Mature, dominant bulls acquire harems during the breeding season. Luckless males without harems are easy to spot; they commiserate in small groups at the edge of the masses. According to Marty Snyderman in *California Marine Life*, "bulls compete only for physical territory, and make no effort to prevent females from breeding with bulls in other areas."

Female California sea lions can reach lengths of six to eight feet and may weigh as much as 250 pounds. Males can reach lengths of eight to ten feet and weigh as much as 700 pounds.

Diving or snorkeling with sea lions is an uncommon experience and I look forward to each encounter.

DICK ANDERSON

Sometimes called the "Mark Twain of diving,"
Dick Anderson is also a true diving pioneer—he
took up scuba in 1948. He has worn many hats
since then: equipment innovator and inventor,
commercial diver, dive instructor, treasure diver,
writer, photographer, and filmmaker. He made
several highly successful, hilarious movies in the
late '60s and early '70s. One of the best known,
Gold from the Winfield Scott, is just as funny now
as it was when it was made. In 1974 Anderson
was part of an operation that recovered an
estimated $1 million in treasure from the Span-
ish galleon *Nuestra Senora de la Maravillas*. Today, Anderson lives in the Los Angeles area and
serves as a diving consultant to an engineering
firm.

I Think That I Shall
Never See A Tank Boot
Square Enough For Me

I could write a book about all the good ideas I've had that didn't sell. Of course, it would have to include the so-so ideas that didn't sell as well as the bum ideas that didn't sell. As a counterbalance, I could also come up with good ideas I've had that did sell. With large print and ample illustrations, it might make sort of a nice pamphlet. One of my nifty ideas was a tank boot.

For the first year or two, U.S. made regulators were sold with a seven-cubic foot tank that had what was termed a "bumped bottom." A bumped bottom tank would stand on end—somewhat precariously—on the rim of the bottom indentation. It seemed that more people liked the bumped bottom than not. Dealers like it because tanks would stand for display. Divers like it because tanks would stand neatly out of the way in the corner of the garage. The main drawback was that tanks liked falling over more than they liked standing up. Tanks on display fell over, usually damaging the attached regulator. The same thing happened on boats when a diver would take his hand off his standing rig for just an instant. Tanks standing in garages also showed a

The tank boot was created to protect the tank and keep it upright–sort of.
Photos by Bonnie J. Cardone.

preference for a horizontal attitude, usually with some damage
to the valve's reserve mechanism.

The bumped bottom tank was superceded by the round
bottom tank. This wasn't done as a measure to prevent tanks
from being stood on end; it was an economic consideration. It
cost an extra buck or so for the tank maker to bump a tank's
bottom. Round bottom tanks inspired the creation of the tank
stand, mainly for dealer display. It was a welcomed development.
Round bottom tanks also inspired the creation of the tank boot—
so the tank would stand up–although the main purpose of a tank
boot, it was said, was to protect the tank.

Tank boots, though similar, had some divergence in design.
Most offered the least footing necessary to keep the tank
standing. It was as though the manufacturers wanted to give you

the option of standing your tank up, but didn't want to make it obvious enough to be interpreted as a recommendation. Booted tanks still preferred the horizontal and would fall over at the slightest provocation.

Memorable tank boots of the past included the soft rubber ones that, through hydraulic ejection, popped off ever so neatly during a high back entry. For a few years they were easier to find on the bottom than rock scallops. But, then they'd be lost again. I'm sure some of those rubber boots had 10 or 15 different owners.

Another boot model, made of plastic, was referred to as the "destroyer." It had six sharp legs that were perfect for ripping through the skin of an inflatable. This boot was also good for tearing holes in station wagon floor mats.

Then there was the "self-destruct" model. Once installed on
a tank it was almost impossible to remove. But, after a few
months the unbreakable plastic would develop a quarter inch
crack and the boot would just fall off.

One of the smartest tank boots I've seen was improvised by
a do-it-yourselfer in Hawaii. His tanks were jammed down into
a six inch length of six inch diameter rubber hose. This provided
a better-than-average base for standing, left the bottom of the
tank open, and protected the tank bottom, too—if tank bottoms
really need protecting.

Not much consideration has ever been given to improving
the marginal standing ability of tank boots. About the only
innovation to come along was the self-draining boot, with a
ribbed interior surface to prevent trapping water against the
tank. This may or may not be an important consideration.
Although I've never had a tank that suffered loss of structural
integrity because of a tank boot, maybe some divers have.

My idea of a tank boot encompassed one completely different consideration. About 10 or 12 years ago a sometime associate, who has a hand in dive equipment manufacture, asked me
to come up with a new and different tank boot. I jumped on it
because I love royalty checks and because I always felt that what
the diving world really needed was a square bottom tank boot.
One of the most annoying things about tanks, besides having
them run low on air, is that they roll around and bang and clank
in your car—and on your boat. How great it would be to have a
square bottom tank boot to discourage rolling.

I got a plastic tank boot and sculpted my boot concept over
it with modeling clay. It had a square bottom with slightly
rounded corners. It also flared out one-half inch to provide
greater standing stability for the tank. (If tank boots weren't

made for standing tanks up they'd be made with round bottoms like the tanks.)

I took my mock-up for review by my sometime associate. Man, was he stoked. He "oohed" and "aaahed" and treated it as though it were the Manhattan Project. He slid it into his office ice box for safekeeping and rubbed his hands together in anticipation. I walked out of his office rubbing my own hands together in anticipation; "Let's see now, 10,000 tank boots at 50 cents per boot. . . ."

That was 10 or 12 years ago. As far as I know my clay mock-up is still in that office ice box. I visit it every year or two.

About three years ago I talked on the phone to a Midwest manufacturer who wanted a new and different boot for his stainless tanks. I told him I had one. He wanted to know what was special about my boot. I couldn't tell him. With no patent protection and no agreement, my claim to the boot could be gone in a sentence. He said he'd get back to me. He didn't.

A guy can only wait so long. I might be dead in another 40 or 50 years. And, I really suspect that the guy who has had my clay mock-up all these years may just be one of those rare individuals who likes having a clay tank boot in his refrigerator. So, that's it folks, Anderson's old/new tank boot is up for grabs. All I want is a small royalty and 12 square bottom boots.

DICK ANDERSON

One Of The Best
Trades I Ever Made

My dive gear always looks kind of well used. With the exception of my wetsuit (I'm a thermal sissy), I use gear until it has almost passed the point of prudent usage. Decked out in my regalia, I look as though I had just spent an hour in a diver tumbler. I never expect to see Mr. Blackwell at 200 feet anyway.

I remember one time when this indifference to glistening diver finery was rewarded in a surprising way. We were anchored at Talcott Shoals off Santa Rosa in California's Channel Islands. The late great skipper Glenn Miller had invited me along on one of his *Coral Sea* dive charters. Thirty feet below was the wreck of the bark *Aggie*. I always get a special kind of fulfillment from finding some brass relic on an old wreck.

While everyone was dressing in, I couldn't help noticing the kid next to me. Boy, did he have some shiny stuff. Some of it was still in boxes. I mean, the stuff looked better than any Christmas morning I ever had. I know the kid sensed, or imagined, a general shipboard awareness that he was somewhat outstanding with his universally new get-up.

I started to strap on my leg knife. It was a knife that only a real mother could love. Its sheath was scratched and gouged to the

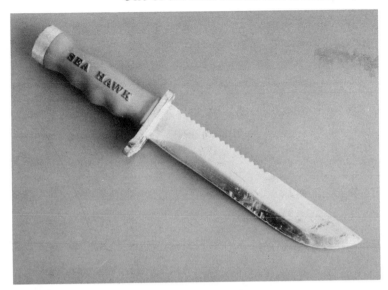

The author is delighted with his trade–a well worn knife like this one is exchanged for a brand new one. Photo by Bonnie J. Cardone.

point where it was only recognizable by its general shape. The blade was dull and blunted from years of indiscriminate probing and prying. The unbreakable plastic handle was starting to crack near the hilt and the butt was an asymmetrical blob of bashed brass. It was a used knife.

Well, that kid spied my knife and asked if he could take a look at it. He handled it the way a museum curator might handle a Faberge Egg, sliding it reverently in and out of the beat-up sheath. "How long have you had it?" he asked. "Oh, about 10 or 15 years, I guess," I said.

The kid reached into his dive bag and pulled out his knife—still in its box. The box was better than my knife. It had four-color printing covering every square inch and even a picture of a celebrity. The knife was even better. It was a "pride of owner-ship" knife. You could tell that because it had its name proudly molded into the handle.

"Want to trade?" the kid asked. I didn't want to take advantage of him so I hesitated for a second or two—but not long enough for him to reconsider. "Well, I'm kind of attached to this knife," I told him. It was the truth. The knife was usually attached to my leg with two straps. But I traded. I'm such a soft touch.

Boy, oh boy! Thirty-five years of diving and my first knife with its own name. I felt just like Errol Flynn or Rex Calibur. And man, did that kid look great with my old knife strapped to his leg. His leg looked like it had been diving for 20 years.

Later that day I watched him use the knife to open a rock scallop and offer a raw slice to his cute, but slightly grimacing, girl buddy. Old as it was, that knife could still slice through a scallop as long as you didn't try to cut cross-grain.

The kid was so pleased with the trade it made me feel like helping him even more. I hinted around a bit that his new tank and regulator looked awfully new and shiny, but he was through trading for the day.

DICK ANDERSON

Abalone Divers
Get My Goat

In 1542, when Juan Cabrillo sailed up the California coast, according to local folklore he left a few domestic goats on some of the Channel Islands. This may have been accidental or it may have been breeding stock for the benefit of later explorations. At any rate, the goats flourished. Unfortunately, translocated animals (including man, as this tale illustrates) often play the roll of biological weeds, surviving at the expense of the native flora and fauna. On San Clemente the U.S. Navy has been waging war with the goats for 50 years or so. The goats may be winning.

On Catalina the problem is handled with less fanfare. In fact, no fanfare at all, as far as I know. There have always been a lot of goats on Catalina, but they're not overrunning the streets of Avalon.

One of the first diving adventure tales that ever inspired me was about a couple of footloose guys who cruised around Catalina, dived all the time, and ate a lot of abalone and lobster. But that isn't all. When these guys craved red meat they'd look for a tender, young kid on a steep cliff over the water. One well aimed shot would cause the kid to fall right into the ocean and the pair would simply cruise over and pull it aboard. That night the kid would serve the purpose its ancestors escaped. It was roasted over a fire and devoured by ravenous seafarers.

I guess this kind of stuff would appeal to a lot of youngsters and I don't feel too guilty about admitting it inspired me some. In those days it sounded a lot better than going to school or getting a job. I never did go out of my way to kill things so it took me a long time to get around to trying a goat dinner.

In the late '50s I hung around occasionally with a couple of actors who liked to dive and cruise around Catalina. One was Dick Norris. Among other things, he is immortalized in that epic, *Beast from 20,000 Fathoms*. He's the picturesque crewman who says, "Gulp!" when the awesome beast swallows him and the aging scientist—diving bell and all. It's the classic understatement of filmdom. The other actor was Britt Lomond. You will remember him as he unlikable Spanish comandante in the Zorro TV series.

No one ever seemed to have any money on these trips. I never had any money to speak of. I'd heard a lot about it but didn't have much actual contact with it. Norris and Lomond never had any money either—that they would admit to anyway. I always had the feeling that each of them got more in unemployment compensation than my annual salary. It didn't seem quite fair because it was my boat we were cruising around on. (And, as a side note: If you've ever owned a boat you know that people who go out on other folks' boats like to feel the gas tank is filled by osmosis.)

Anyway, one long weekend we three cruised over to Avalon. Always short of money, we were going to live off the fat of the land. After a lot of lobster and abalone (an instance of overlapping seasons, I better add), we decided it was time for some red meat procured in the classic cliff-shot manner. But, by the time we actually got around to doing it, Norris and Lomond had developed other interests. The worldly demeanor of those two glib actors was just too much for the Avalon beach girls to resist and the guys couldn't bear to pull themselves away. "You go get the goat, Anderson, we'll interview some cooks," they said.

I was more hungry than lonely anyway. A roasting kid seemed pretty appealing right then. I rowed out to my boat and cruised down to the East End. Here, steep cliffs rise above the water and a narrow rocky beach. I spotted three goats on the face of the cliff; one tender looking kid, one chewy looking nanny and a grizzly old ram. I drew a bead on the kid and squeezed off a shot. Missed!

The kid scampered up and over the crest of the cliff before I could even recock. The nanny wasn't waiting around either. I got off one more shot before she jumped out of sight. A clean miss. Dinner was disappearing fast. The two shots finally got the attention of the big ram. He turned his head slowly and looked at me. Then he began plodding carefully up the cliff. His ancestors had once escaped from Juan Cabrillo and he wasn't too worried about me.

Now, I had always heard that kids were tender and delicious; that young nannies were OK and that old rams were tough as tires. But, hunger has a way of diminishing the negative aspects of the hunt. I figured if I bagged the ram we could pound the steaks like abalone and eat for a month. I sighted in on the ram and fired. Whap! The ram froze for an instant and then peeled off into space. He didn't splash into the water as the old scenario related; he crashed down onto the rocky beach. I couldn't just drive the boat over and hoist him aboard. I'd have to anchor and go get him.

The anchorage in that immediate area isn't very good. The

bottom is shallow and sandy. I had to let out a lot of scope on the anchorline to get a good hook-up. Another problem was getting the ram out to the boat. I wasn't sure he would float so I got out a BC to put on him. Then I stripped to my shorts and swam to shore.

That goat was a lot bigger than I thought. I mean, he weighed something like 200 pounds. It was a real effort just to drag the carcass down the sloping beach. I put the BC on the goat, fastened it securely and blew it full of air. Then I dragged the ram out as far as I could and started swimming. It wasn't easy. That goat was big and heavy and had a lot of resistance in the water. I couldn't get a good kick either, because his legs were in the way. Thoughts of hungry sharks began to erode my waning macho.

Then, quite suddenly, the afternoon surface chop came up, along with a brisk breeze. I began inhaling a lot of water. Next, I was startled almost into coronary arrest by a sudden bump on the leg and dark shapes zipping through the chalky water around me. Sharks, I thought and released the goat. It wasn't sharks. It was a group of curious sea lions. At that point I was nearing the low ebb of my goat meat enthusiasm. I grabbed a massive horn and resumed swimming. Somehow I wasn't having much fun. Instead of getting closer, the boat seemed to be getting farther away. The wind was pushing the boat to the opposite end of its anchorline radius. It was a long, hard swim.

By the time I got the goat to the boat I had sucked in so much sea water, and was so overexerted, I was almost sick. I climbed aboard and really strained to get the goat up and over the gunwale. It was hopeless. I was just too worn out and weak to get him aboard. And, that poor soggy goat smelled so strong I did get sick, really sick. As my stomach heaved in protest, I just let go of the goat and collapsed on the deck for five or ten minutes.

After I regained my composure and pulled anchor, the goat, along with my BC, was lost in a sea of whitecaps.

Back in Avalon it took a while to locate Norris and Lomond and their fan club. "Where's the goat, Anderson?" they asked in unison. I told them the story. They didn't believe me. It became a running gag that went on all evening. We were still arguing about it at 10:00 that night when we went into the Marlin Club. As usual it was noisy but this evening the noise was mainly concentrated on two slightly inebriated abalone divers who were trying their best to convince a houseful of unbelieving patrons that they had just found a 200 pound goat, five miles at sea, wearing a BC.

"Do You Dive A Lot?"
A Wreck, a Rock, And
a Raisin . . . with Legs

A while back I got a call from a mystery man I'll call the Mystery Man. He wanted an honest, reliable diver to make a quick dip to verify a treasure laden Spanish galleon. The wreck was clear to-hell-and-gone on the other side of Catalina Island and clear to-hell-and-gone under 250 feet of blue Pacific water. How or why it got there was anybody's guess. I told the Mystery Man I was honest and reliable but I didn't want to lie to him too much right off. We met to talk it over.

After giving me the run-down, but not showing me the treasure map, he offered me the choice of cash payment or a piece of the action. To make that offer even more appealing, he hinted that they might need a salvage divemaster when they started working the wreck. I opted for the cash. A date was set.

In preparation I yanked two sets of doubles from under my workbench and hooked up a regulator; they had 3,000 psi and air that was as fresh as that in Yosemite on a spring morning.

We cruised to the site in a sleek 40 foot Baglietto. I hardly ever get the chance to bang up a boat that good. On most of the boats I dive from the skipper wouldn't care if you chopped wood on deck. This skipper was so shipshape he thought I should be wearing Sperry Topsiders instead of Chippewa engineer boots. He followed me around with a wiping cloth.

South of Catalina we slowed and metered the site. The galleon was there all right, a pronounced ten foot lump on the flat bottom. Down went the hook, the white nylon fading into the clear blue about one-half mile under the bow.

As I donned my regalia, the Mystery Man repeated his offer of a piece of the action instead of cash. I was glad he was talking "cash." One can't be too sure about checks from mystery men. I stuck with the cash. Meanwhile, the Mystery Man was eye-balling my double tank rig.

"Do you dive a lot?" he asked, leaning over my tanks. "Hell yes," I said, "Cousteau and I sort of started out together." I was leaning over the cap rail, tracing the descent of the fading anchorline. I was thinking that if I wasn't so greedy I'd have some other nitwit to share this adventure with me.

The Mystery Man was leaning closer over my tanks, peering at something. "How often do you dive?" he asked. "All the time," I answered, a little annoyed. This was a hell of a time to be checking my credentials. He was so intent on my tanks I just had to look myself. There were three black widow spiders housed between the tanks; two in one set and one in the other. And, there were enough little round eggs to produce 200 or 300 more. What could I say?

The fastidious skipper headed for the cabin and started rummaging through cabinets looking for a can of bug spray. I put on the double spider rig and jumped over the side. The spiders went with me. The Mystery Man was torn between watching me or the skipper, who was busy practicing overkill.

After returning from his dive and taking off his scuba tanks, the author finds three dead black widow spiders–that look very much like raisins. Photo by Bonnie J. Cardone.

Down, down, down I went, swimming at first, then dropping like a rock as my 3/8 inch suit compressed and lost buoyancy. Being a man of great courage when I'm not scared, I suppressed that feeling of uneasiness one sometimes gets when one can't see anything but water above or below.

A hazy, mottled pattern began to take shape below and I squeezed a shot of air into my BC. I landed right on top of the galleon. It looked a lot like a rock. It felt like a rock. It was a rock.

I swam a big circle, keeping the anchorline in sight, to make sure I was on the right galleon. I was. Suddenly the cold hit me. My full 3/8 inch suit was a solid 1/16 inch thick at that depth. I had no thrilling find to keep me warm. Then some automatic urgency aimed me at the anchorline and whispered, "Anderson, get your dumb buns out of here!" I started my ascent, having discovered nothing more exciting than that there are a lot of fair sized lingcod on the deep rocks on the other side of Catalina.

Was the Mystery Man disappointed? You bet. His brain was telling him I had found the galleon but was keeping it a secret until I could come back later with Mel Fisher and salvage it without him. He said he was coming back with a real diver next time. I asked him if he could swim. The skipper went to make coffee.

I spotted one of the black widows lying on deck in a puddle of bug spray. He, or she, more correctly, looked like a raisin with legs—completely ruined. The other two were dead as well. They probably drowned, but I'm not sure. I have no idea how long black widows can hold their breaths. It could have been a spider embolism or the bends for all I know. Maybe the cold got to them. Anyway, few spiders get that kind of spur-of-the-moment adventure. They were taking their chances and just got unlucky.

We upped anchor and headed for home. All adventures

can't be grand ones. Actually, I felt lucky to get my hands on the few begrudged $100 bills. Had I been more of a gambler I would have ended up with a piece of the rock!

E.R. CROSS

Chronicling the lifetime activities of Ellis Royal Cross would result in a book longer than *Gone with the Wind*. The man (he was 76 when this was written) is never still and never at a loss for something to do. Ideas continually whirl around in his brain and he is always in the thick of something. Cross has been a commercial diver, diving educator, underwater photographer, environmentalist, and marine consultant. He also served in the U.S. Navy for 14 years. Cross is a prolific author with several books to his credit and numerous articles. He has written the Technifacts column for *Skin Diver Magazine* since 1964.

E.R. CROSS

Halfway to Hell

should have known. Any diving job that had to be done in the middle of the hottest, windiest, dustiest, damnedest desert in Utah must be something besides routine. I should have known and given the two pulls on my lifeline that would drop me back to the bottom of the cool Pacific Ocean. I was placing dynamite in a wreck 80 feet under when my tender called me topside to take a call from Green River, Utah, via the San Pedro marine radio operator. Over the radio-telephone the representative of the Vitro Uranium Company assured me, "The job is in only 43 feet of water."

"What do I do when I get to the bottom?" This to me was more important than where or how deep. "All you have to do is hook onto a pump so we can raise it to the surface for repairs," was the reassuring reply.

For this they were willing to pay me $500. It sounded like an easy, one day job. By using self contained diving equipment I could work alone. No standby diver and no tender. I wouldn't have to split the five bills I'd get for the job. This I liked. I took the job, telling the worried official I'd be there ready for work the next morning. While I had a cup of coffee I thought of all the ways I could spend that easy money. I went back to work on the wreck.

It took only a few minutes to put the detonator in the dynamite charge I had placed earlier. When I was back topside, and the diving boat in the clear, the charge was set off and I headed for Los Angeles harbor.

Two hours later at the International Airport, Western Air Lines told me Green River was about halfway between Salt Lake City and Boulder City, Colorado. Their earliest flight was to Boulder City. After I had checked two complete diving rigs, three spare cylinders, a wet and a dry type diving suit, and a Cornelius high pressure air compressor through on my ticket as excess baggage, I was glad I was to be reimbursed for all my travel expenses. I had time for a drink to the success of Vitro and then boarded the plane.

At Boulder City, trouble, in minor form as yet, became my partner. Trouble was the only partner I had from then until the diving job was finished. Cecil Smith, the mining engineer for the uranium company, met the plane and helped me load my diving outfit in his car for the 90 mile drive to Green River. Smith, young, tanned, and energetic, was a product of the atomic age and the uranium hunt that had resulted. Always he seemed to be late or hurrying desperately so he wouldn't be. When the car was loaded he said, "The roads between here and town are being repaired." Then, as an afterthought "We'll have to hurry."

To Smith "hurry" meant just that. Several thousand bumps, five jackrabbits, and one sage hen later we arrived at Green River. Beyond this enterprising, unincorporated bit of Utah the roads became two lane trails. When we finally arrived at the mine I welcomed any excuse to get out of the desert tortured car. That is I welcomed anything except the diving job I found waiting for me.

Now I knew. The fine print in the deal had been omitted during our conversation over the ship-to-shore telephone. Maybe

E.R. Cross and the portable compressor that kept his scuba tanks filled with air during the Utah mine project.

the uranium company hadn't hit pay dirt yet and couldn't afford to stay on the air waves long enough to give me all the information. Also, maybe someone was afraid I wouldn't accept the job if I had the straight dope. As far as he had gone, the representative of the mining company had been right. He just hadn't talked long enough. True the water was only 43 feet deep. But it was at the bottom of a mine shaft four feet square and more than 350 feet deep in the desert.

One thing was sure. I wouldn't have trouble finding the

pump because it was a big, 16 stage job nearly two feet in diameter and weighing half a ton. It almost completely filled the mine shaft. According to Smith the pump was lashed to large timbers with chains. The timbers were braced across a frame work holding the mine cribbing. Whenever I was ready to make a dip all I had to do was descend, secure a lifting cable to the pump, squeeze past the pump in one corner of the shaft, cut the chains, and then surface so the pump could be hoisted out and repaired. Considerably different from the first description of the job, but still not a bad one, provided everything went as it was supposed to by the company script.

There were two ways to get up and down in the mine shaft. Either we had to climb 300 feet of ladder with man locks and small landings every 20 feet, or we could ride the ore bucket that was normally used to haul uranium ore to the surface. The bucket, or skip, was raised and lowered by a winch at the surface which was operated by an ex-cowboy whose entire vocabulary, complete with a Texas twang, was "reckon so," and "mebbe." For obvious reasons he was known as Tex. I never was able to find out for sure whether or not the winch and cable met Utah mining safety standards.

While I was checking out the equipment, Bruce Hanson, chief geologist at the mine, came over from the cook shack. According to him the water in the mine was cold. I estimated about three or four hours of underwater work plus another hour or two in the shaft at the water's surface getting things ready. I didn't want to expend half my energy shivering from the cold water so I put on a wet type diver's suit and then a drysuit.

As we loaded the diving equipment and spare cylinders into the ore bucket, Smith checked me out on the signal system to the winch operator. "One bell means lower away, two bells means

E.R. Cross gives last minute instructions to the miners as he pulls on one of the two suits he wore while diving in the Utah Mine.

hoist," he explained. "If you want Tex to hoist or lower at dead slow speed, give him three bells followed by the direction you want the hoist to go. One bell when the hoist is in operation means stop," he concluded.

"That's fine," I said, as I climbed into the ore skip already half full of diving equipment, "But how do I ring the bell?"

Smith climbed in behind me with complete disregard for the diving equipment on which he landed. He reached into the corner of the shaft and gave a mighty pull on a wire there. I heard the ear-splitting clang of a large bell as we dropped rapidly into the dark. Thirty feet down we passed Hanson and one of the miners. They were in a man lock at the side of the main shaft climbing down the seemingly endless ladder. They would help

E.R. Cross loads scuba equipment in an ore bucket just before being lowered 300 feet down into a uranium mine shaft. His job was to secure a cable to a water pump so it could be hoisted out of the mine and repaired.

rig equipment when they reached the bottom, or surface of the water.

As we neared the bottom of the mine, torrents of water pouring down on us made conversation difficult. I shouted into Smith's ear, "This reminds me of the tropical rains we had in the South Pacific."

"Yes," was his reply, "but rain doesn't have arsenic in it."

"Arsenic?" I yelled.

"Sure. Remember the bones of the cattle we saw as we came

out to the mine? They died when they drank some of this water that we pumped to the surface."

I liked this job less by the minute. I knew now what the funny taste was in the water. I also knew that I usually got some water in my mouth from around the regulator mouthpiece and decided I was going to be pretty close mouthed for the duration of this job. A zero behind the $500 would have helped about then.

When my mask, regulator, cylinder, and flashlight were out of the skip, Smith gave two sharp pulls on the signal wire. Almost immediately the ore bucket was raised above me. When it was clear he gave another pull and the ascent stopped. Now any falling rocks would be stopped by the bucket.

I could think of nothing more to keep me out of the water so I slid in and under the surface. Immediately, the dim light from Smith's lamp was blotted out. The underwater light I carried was invisible when more than two inches from my mask.

I slid slowly down the planks forming the cribbing, feeling my way with light touches against the sides of the shaft. When I drifted away from the side I was in black space with no reference points to guide me. There was no up nor down, only complete, crushing blackness, and a sense of timelessness and weightlessness.

My feet brushed lightly against some object. I felt carefully with my feet and legs. As I inched slowly down I could make out the pump, the cross timbers, and the discharge hose from the pump to the surface. Going deeper, and by feeling carefully around the entire area, I was able, after a few minutes, to identify all parts of the pump and the rigging that held it in place. There was one object through the lifting bridle of the pump that Smith had not told me about. It felt like a long length of six inch diameter pipe. I felt along the pipe to where it was bedded into a small pocket in the solid rock through which the shaft passed at this point.

Suddenly, with no warning, my regulator began exhausting air at a terrific rate. Dirt in the water pouring down on the equipment as we descended into the mine had worked into the valve system and had blocked the high pressure valve open. This allowed great quantities of air to be discharged into the water. I knew I had only a few minutes' air supply left. I felt along the other end of the pipe trying to complete the inspection before I had to ascend. The pipe did not end where it should have but extended up into some type of opening through the side of the shaft. I crawled up into this opening for several feet and still did not find the end of the pipe.

Air was coming to me very slowly now and I knew my supply was exhausted. I started back down the pipe toward the shaft. The increasing water pressure shut my air off completely. My life was now on a minute to minute basis. Now without air I scrambled through the timbers jutting out from the pump support. I tore my way through the discharge hose and electric wire leading to the pump, then over debris nearly filling the shaft. Desperately in need of air I finally reached a clear space and started up. It seemed an eternity before my scuba grudgingly gave me a small breath of air, not enough to completely replace the foul air in my lungs, but enough to support life for another minute. Two more small whispers of air were released into my starved lungs and then I was at the surface.

Smith and Hanson and the miner, now at the water level, helped me from the water. When I quit gasping for air I told them about the pipe that held the pump down. While Hanson got the rest of my diving equipment out of the skip, Smith and I tried to figure how to get the pipe out of the way so the pump could be

It was important not to imbibe any of the mine shaft water because it was contaminated with arsenic.

raised. Even if I was able to cut the chain that held the pump to the timbers, it could not be lifted until the pipe was removed. But first we had to get the half ton weight of the pump off the pipe. This we could do with the hoist. Then, if I could work the pipe up and out the small shaft into which it extended, I would have it made.

With a new regulator and tank of air on and tested, I slid into the blackness and down to the submerged pump. I made a quick descent this time because I knew my way through the maze of equipment and because I carried a large, heavy pair of bolt cutters with which to snap the chain. In position on the pump, I felt around in the corner of the shaft for the wire that led up through the water to the signal bell on the surface. When I found the wire I grabbed it firmly and gave three hard pulls. I had no way of knowing whether or not the bell had even worked but I "reckoned" "mebbe" Tex would heed the warning to go slow and gave one more hard pull. I felt a slight vibration as the skip started down to me.

When I had the hoisting cable clamped to the pump, I tried to get to the chain so I could cut it loose with the bolt cutters. The way the chain and the pump were rigged it was impossible to reach a place in the chain where a cut could be made unless I could get underneath the pump. When I squeezed under the pump I found there wasn't room to work the four-foot bolt cutters. I squirmed back up above the pump. By standing on my head and reaching down past the pump I found I could just reach the chain. I got one link between the jaws and slowly forced the cutters shut. One half of the link parted. One more cut and this would all be over with.

But I couldn't reach the cut to locate the opposite side of the link. I worked deeper along the pump until I could run my finger along the chain links to find the one that was partly cut. When I did find it I still couldn't hold my finger on the cut link and also put the bolt cutters in place on the opposite side. I made a couple of cuts on what I hoped was the right link but the chain still held. I squirmed a little deeper, still upside down. The scuba cylinder was now wedged into a corner where the virgin rock and the planking of the cribbing met. The pump was slightly above me, the bottom flange pushed into my chest hard enough to keep me from getting a full breath of air.

Now I could reach one of the cut links with both hands. Guiding the bolt cutters into place I began trying to squeeze the handles together. I couldn't exert enough pressure to make the cut. By turning slightly to one side I was able to rest one handle of the cutter against the rock and to push on the other. This worked and I felt the link sheer. At the same instant the weight of the pump, previously held by the chain, swung into me and crushed me against the side of the shaft. I gasped for a breath of air, fighting to keep the mouthpiece between my teeth and free of water. I was trapped, held solidly against the rough rock of the mine shaft. As I talked myself into calmer thinking I suddenly realized that the rocks against which I was smashed felt hot compared with the temperature of the water. The thought flashed through my mind, "As hot as these rocks are I must be halfway to hell." Then a sobering realization struck me—if I didn't get out of here soon I'd be a lot closer to hell than anyone on earth knew.

Calmer now, I realized that a plank on one side of the shaft was gouging into my side. Also I found I still clung to the bolt cutters. I couldn't reach the signal wire that lead to the surface. Probably wouldn't dare use it if I could. I couldn't push the tremendous weight of the pump away from me. With solid rock behind me, my only hope was to loosen the plank that was digging into my right side. If I could move the plank, I might squeeze past the pump and get to the surface. I strained against the plank until my ears rang with the exertion and a need for more air. No matter now hard I pushed, the plank held firmly.

Then I remembered the heavy bolt cutters. I might beat the plank loose with them. I felt along the plank until I found a place where it was spiked to the timber and began beating with the cutters. When I checked the plank hadn't loosened at all. I was getting weak and dizzy from being upside down for so long and from not getting enough air. If I didn't get out of here soon I'd be too weak to make it at all. Gasping for air I again smashed at the plank with the bolt cutters. After several more minutes I again felt the plank. It had moved slightly but the heavy spikes still held. A few more weakening smashes with the cutters, rest, smash, rest, and then smash again, and I finally felt one end of the plank loosen. But, not enough for me to squeeze by. I was too weak to continue beating but if I could move the one free end of the plank to one side, even a little way, I could get free. With the cutters as a lever, I began prying against the plank, trying to force it along the rough surface of the rock and to one side. Inch by inch it gave until I was halfway through the small opening. Finally, by prying against the plank, and with this force to squeeze me between the pump and the plank, I exhaled completely and gave a mighty heave. As I slid through the small space the bolt cutters dropped from my numb hand, clattered against the pump once, and then dropped silently to the bottom of the mine shaft.

Half unconscious but now getting air, I started toward the surface. Suddenly I remembered the ore bucket above me. I couldn't get past the skip because it completely filled the shaft. The only way to the surface and help was to go into one of the small man locks, up the underwater ladder, through a small man hole, and then back into the mine shaft through the next man lock above the bucket. I rested for a few minutes, hoping I could squeeze through the small man hole without taking off my diving equipment. I'd had enough of life under the surface of arsenic filled water. I worked my way slowly up the ladder to the man hole. It was going to be a tight squeeze to get through. First I put one arm through the hole. Then my head. By turning sideways so the cylinder was in a corner, I was able to force my way through. Now I would make it. I finally reached the surface of the water, again needing help to get out.

Since I had started diving the water in the shaft had risen

about five feet. The landing was now under a foot of water. Wearily I removed my mask and tank and sat down. The back of my diving suit was ripped to shreds. When I leaned back against the dripping bulkhead I could feel water trickle down my spine. I wasn't sure whether it was the cold water or the thought of going back down to finish the job that caused the cold shivers to shake me. I turned to Smith, "Let's take a pull on the pump with the lifting wire," I shouted above the noise of the water, "Then we can tell what we have to do to get the pump up."

For reply he reached over and grabbed the signal wire. When he was sure all the men were clear he gave three pulls on the wire followed by two pulls. Slowly the lifting cables tightened. Then they jerked slightly as something came loose below. But almost immediately the wire tightened and would not budge. One bell was given on the signal wire to stop the lift before something snapped.

Wearily I told Smith, "Get me another tank of air." While he was getting the cylinder from the next man lock above us I removed the regulator from the other unit. When all was ready and the equipment tested, I put it on and reluctantly descended to the top of the ore bucket. From there I went into the man lock and to the small man hole through which I had to squeeze. This time I took a few minutes and pried two of the boards off the edge of the hatch. This made the opening large enough so I could slip through easily and reach the pump with no difficulty.

I found the pump was now pulled up so tightly against the pipe that it couldn't be moved. I located the signal wire and gave three bells followed by one. The pump lowered slowly. When the pipe felt clear, I gave a sharp tug on the wire and the lowering stopped. I still could not get the pipe loose. It was wedged against a water soaked board and half of a 50 gallon steel drum. Where did these damned things come from? More to the point, what was I going to do with them? I couldn't drop them to the bottom of the shaft because they wouldn't clear the small space between the pump and the side. I didn't want to put them in the man lock because my way to the surface would then be blocked.

I decided the only answer was to take them, one at a time, to the surface and let the crew there dispose of them. The next problem was getting them through the hatch and to the surface. Nearly an hour later my scuba cylinder was again almost empty, but both the drum and the plank were out of the way. I surfaced to get another cylinder of air. Smith suggested we call it a day. When he told me it was 4:30, I agreed. This had been one hell of a day.

Early the next morning, stiff and sore from being pushed around by the pump, I came out to the mine. I started the Cornelius compressor and began filling the air cylinders. By 9:30 the tanks were filled and the desert sun had baked some of the soreness from my battered muscles. I dressed into the rubber suits I had repaired the night before. The crew loaded the equipment into the bucket. Then we all climbed in and started for the bottom. We found the water had risen another eight feet during the night. I now had 60 feet of water to work in, a depth requiring decompression to prevent bends if diving time was too great.

When I had my gear on and was ready to descend, Hanson checked me out on the layout of the mine shaft and tunnels. According to him the small tunnel into which the pipe had been pushed was the loading chute that ran down at an angle from the floor of the main tunnel to the mine shaft. Uranium ore, dumped from the ore cars into the chute, slid down into the ore skip, which was lowered until it was just under the bottom of the chute.

If I could get the pipe at just the right angle I could slide it back up the chute into the main tunnel. It would then be clear of the pump. This was the plan I thought over as I descended to the submerged pump.

When I reached the pump I located the signal wire that led to the surface and gave three pulls followed by one. Again I could feel the vibrations as Tex, 300 feet above me, lowered the ore bucket. This time I had no trouble finding the wire and stopped the skip when a few feet of slack was available to attach to the pump. When the cable was clamped to the pump I gave the signal for dead slow hoist away. Keeping one hand on the pump so I could feel the movements, and the other firmly gripping the signal wire, I waited for the slack to be taken up and the pump lifted slightly. When the pipe was loose, I signaled for Tex to stop, holding the pump in position. Then I tried to work the pipe up the incline of the chute and out of the lifting bridle of the pump. It would only go a foot or two, not enough to clear the pump. Finally, I forced my way past the pipe into the small chute until I was above the end of the pipe.

Slowly I was able to work the pipe up the chute until I felt something stop my movements. I felt around and discovered a grating over the upper end of the chute. Hanson had forgotten to tell me the chute had been blocked off. I braced myself and shoved up. All I could succeed in doing was to crimp off my air supply. I shifted position until I could again get air. Either the wood of the grating had swelled when the mine flooded or a workman had left an ore car stopped over the grating. Finally, I worked the pipe into position so that I could slide it up until it struck the grating. I banged away at the wood until my arms ached with weariness. At the rate I was using up air I would be out in another few minutes. I rested for a minute, then renewed

The ore bucket, with the water pump attached to it by chains, is raised above the mine shaft.

ramming the grating with the pipe. Finally the wood in one corner splintered, then gave way completely as the tension on it was released. I reached up and pushed the grating aside, then pushed the pipe up into the tunnel and out of the way. The pump could now be lifted.

I felt my way along the tunnel until I came to the mine shaft, clawed my way up the side of the skip, then into the man lock and up until I was clear to ascend. When I reached the surface Smith gave Tex the signal to hoist away slow. We waited to see if all was clear. When the skip reached our level the signal was given to stop hoisting. We loaded the diving equipment into the bucket, then raised the skip until the pump was clear of the water. The pump had to be re-rigged before it could be lifted topside. They didn't need me. I started climbing the 300 feet of ladder out of that hell-hole to the best damned heat, wind, and dust in the world.

Deep Rescue

In a short period of history, thousands of submarines have been built, almost exclusively as combat vessels. Many have been lost in action. A few have suffered peacetime disasters in which all hands were lost. Even fewer have been sunk but with some of the crew escaping or being rescued. One such disaster was the sinking of the USS *Squalus* off Portsmouth, New Hampshire, on May 23, 1939.

This is the story of the *Squalus* and how the heroic efforts of a few men saved some of their shipmates and of the divers who rescued those men from a depth of 242 feet of bitterly cold water.

The *Squalus* was the Navy's newest S-type submarine, 310 feet long and designed for fleet service. She displaced 1,450 tons and had been constructed at the Portsmouth Navy Yard. She was launched there on September 14, 1938, and commissioned in March of 1939. Full scale sea trials were started on May 15.

One test the boat had to pass for acceptance was to go from cruising on the surface, under simulated wartime conditions at full speed (about 16 knots), to a depth of 50 feet in 60 seconds. A few days earlier she had missed passing this crash dive test by five seconds.

Early on the bright sunny Tuesday morning of May 23,

Lieutenant Oliver Naquin, captain of the *Squalus*, got his vessel underway and proceeded out into the choppy North Atlantic to a stretch of deep water off the Isle of Shoals to try to put the *Squalus* through this test successfully.

When operating on the surface the *Squalus* was powered by four diesel engines that drew air for their operation from a 31 inch diameter main induction valve and piping system, the opening of which was high up under the bridge deck just aft the conning tower. A second air induction system, this one 18 inches in diameter, provided air for the crew compartments throughout the boat when it was on the surface. Valves that closed these air induction systems were operated by a man in the control room.

Small, heavy doors, each only two and one-half by three feet, in all watertight bulkheads, were open but guarded by a man whose sole duty was to close the door quickly if an emergency developed. At operation stations throughout the boat telephone talkers were in direct communication with the captain's talker in the control room.

At 0813 Lt. Naquin sent a radio message to the Navy Yard telling them where he would start his test dive. The *Squalus* carried 56 experienced Navy personnel and three civilian technicians from the Navy Yard; a total crew of 59.

At 0839 all hands had reported to their dive stations ready for diving. Lt. Doyle, the executive officer, was in the control room with the team of ten men it took to operate the many valves and fittings required to keep the *Squalus* cruising under wartime conditions. He reported to Lt. Naquin, who was still on the bridge, that the boat was ready for diving. The captain informed the Navy Yard, advising that he was on station and preparing to submerge for one hour.

In the control room, the "Christmas tree," an array of lights showing the condition of dozens of valves, fittings, and openings throughout the boat (red lights for open, green lights for closed) showed all green except eight red lights; four for the exhausts for the engines, one for the flapper valve through which the radio antenna rose, and one for the conning tower hatch leading to the bridge where Lt. Naquin and two men remained. The final two red lights were for the two high induction valves that would remain open until the *Squalus* began her glide below the surface.

Still on the bridge, Lt. Naquin gave the order, "Stand by to dive."

The loud blare of the klaxons gave the crew the first warning of the dive. Then, following the two crewmen, Naquin slipped through the hatch leading below to the conning tower and, with the help of one man, closed and dogged it. One red light on the control panel went out and one green light came on. In the radio room the radioman completed sending the dive information message and retracted the radio antenna. A green light replaced another red light. The skipper dropped down the ladder into the control room.

Time: 0840 and 0 seconds.

Lt. Naquin gave the order, "Take her down," and started his stopwatch. The second blare of the klaxons warned the crew the boat was on her way down.

0840 and 5 seconds.

Control Room—The diving officer already had bow planes placed at hard dive so the bow would be dragged down. He now ordered, "Floor number one and two main ballast tanks." The flooded tanks would provide neutral buoyancy so the bow planes could do their job.

0840 and 10 seconds.

Control Room—The diving officer ordered flood valves open on number three and four main ballast tanks, leaving vents closed. When the Christmas tree indicated the boat was tight he would open the vents. Cruising power was now shifted to electric motors and the four diesels were shut down and their exhausts closed. Four more lights went from red to green. Only two lights remained red; the two high air induction valves were still open. Alfred Prien, operating the control board, now pulled the two levers that caused the air induction valves to close. The last two red lights winked out and green lights flashed on. The board indicated the boat was tight.

0840 and 25 seconds.

Control Room—Lt. Doyle ordered vents opened on number three and four main ballast tanks. Depth gauges read 28 feet and five seconds later, 30 feet.

0840 and 40 seconds.

Control Room—Depth, 40 feet.

0840 and 50 seconds.

Main Induction Valves—Water was over the top of the two valves. The 18 inch valve was closed but the 31 inch main valve had not closed; it was wide open and water was rushing into the valve and through the piping toward the engine room and after compartments.

0841 and 0 seconds.

Control Room—Depth gauges read 50 feet. Lt. Naquin and the civilian technician stopped their watches and the skipper was congratulated. He had made his 60 second dive.

Engine Room—The telephone talker screamed into the telephone, "Water flooding engine room."

0841 and 5 seconds.

Control Room—Further word came from the engine room. "Induction opened. Take her up." Lt. Naquin ordered, "Blow all ballast." Then he added, "Blow all buoyancy."

0841 and 15 seconds.

Control Room—The stern of the *Squalus* was now settling rapidly. Lt. Naquin ordered full power on the electric motors. The boat steadied for a moment, then continued to settle by the stern. Alfred Prien, at the controls, was still trying to pull the lever controlling the main induction valve farther back. It was as far as it would go. All lights were still green.

Forward Torpedo Room—Lt. Nichols and his crew closed watertight doors leading from their compartment. They were sealed in.

After Engine Room—Lloyd Mannes, guard at the bulkhead door between the engine room and the control room, suddenly saw a head of water racing toward his station. He started to close the door.

0841 and 30 seconds.

Control Room—Ten men and two officers frantically operated all valves and fittings, trying desperately to bring the stricken *Squalus* back to the surface. The stern of the vessel was now down nearly 30 degrees and still sinking. The electric drive motors slowed to a stop, shorted out by the rising salt water. The lights on the Christmas tree, still all green, flickered and went out. The *Squalus* was going to go all the way to the bottom.

Engine Room—The telephone talker screamed, "Take her up. Take her up. Water flooding...." The telephone system went dead.

Forward Battery Compartment—Chief Gainer secured his watertight door, sealing himself in the electric control room above the battery compartment. His instruments showed a dead short in the system. At the risk of his life he opened the hatch and climbed quickly down into the battery compartment. Great blue flames of electricity were flashing across batteries and fittings. It was so hot the rubber cases of the batteries were melting. If that happened they could explode with enough force to blow the sub to bits. In the midst of the heat and flashes of electricity, he managed to pull the two main switches. Lights, already dim and flickering, went out in the forward compartments of the *Squalus*.

Engine Room—Lloyd Mannes, in the act of closing the water-tight door, saw four men struggling through rising water trying to reach safety. He waited. First Radioman Arthur Booth made it through.

0841 and 40 seconds.

Engine Room—Blanchard made it through the door into the control room. Isaacs was still fighting forward. Mannes reached out and pulled him sprawling into the control room. Half swimming through the rising water, Pharmacist's Mate Raymond O'Hara, still ten feet away from the door, screamed, "Leave it open. Leave it open." Slipping and falling through the rising water, he was just able to grasp the hatch combing and pull himself through into the control room. Now, with water lapping over the raised hatch combing, Mannes had to literally lift the 200 pound steel door closed since the *Squalus* was now bow-up at about a 40 degree angle.

0841 and 50 seconds.

Control Room—A flashlight was held up to the glass port in the door Mannes had just closed. Oily water crept up and across it. The sub was passing 90 feet, still bow up at about 45 degrees.

0843 and 0 seconds.

Control Room—All lights were out. Emergency lanterns and flashlights provided a dim glow in the control room. *Squalus* was passing 185 feet, then 200, and 220.

0845 and 0 seconds.

Control Room—The *Squalus* gently touched the muddy bottom stern first and a few seconds later the bow settled into the mud at a depth of 242 feet.

Lt. Naquin tried to reach each after compartment by emergency sound powered telephone. There was no reply. He next tapped on the closed forward battery room door. There was an answering tap and the door was slowly opened. "How is the forward torpedo room," the skipper asked. Someone answered, "All dry and doors secured, sir." That was that. The control room and the two forward compartments were dry. There were 28 crewmen, three officers, and one civilian technician alive in the forward compartments. Apparently all compartments aft were flooded. There were 23 crewmen, one officer and two civilian technicians in those compartments.

Lt. Naquin now began emergency procedures from within the sunken *Squalus* that might make rescue possible. First he ordered the release of the forward telephone rescue buoy. The release lever was pulled and the buoy floated to the surface on the end of 325 feet of steel wire. Next, a red smoke bomb was released. This floated to the surface, bobbed clear of the water, then splashed back, leaving a thick red smudge of smoke spreading over the water. Now all they could do was wait.

Inside the sub were cylinders of oxygen for breathing and soda lime to absorb exhaled carbon dioxide. For the present, Lt. Naquin ruled out using the individual Momsen escape lungs because of the extreme depth and the cold. Inside the sub the crew could survive for up to five days. But it was going to be a very cold wait. The water temperature outside was 30°F. The submarine had no power, no heat, and only one small emergency locker of food. A ten gallon can of emergency water was stowed in each

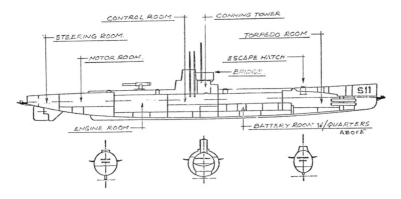

Layout of a Squalus *type submarine. Illustration by B. Cooper.*

compartment. Air was their most precious resource. To conserve this as much as possible each crew member was assigned a spot in the boat, given blankets for warmth, and told to lie down and to limit talking to essential orders.

By 1100, operation officers at the sub base were worrying about not having heard from the *Squalus*. They reported this to the commandant of the yard who then initiated emergency procedures to try to locate the *Squalus*. The *Sculpin*, sister ship to the *Squalus*, was ordered to sea to locate the missing sub.

At 1240, four hours after the dive started, a sixth smoke bomb was released. On board the *Sculpin*, Lt. Denby glanced back in the direction from which they had come and saw the smoke. The *Sculpin* made a quick turn and headed in that direction. Soon the crew of the *Sculpin* spotted the telephone and rescue buoy. The men in the *Squalus* heard the sounds of the *Sculpin's* propellers and another smoke bomb was released, this one spreading the red smudge directly in front of the *Sculpin*. Carefully the *Sculpin* was brought alongside the telephone buoy and it was lifted aboard. For half a minute they were in direct communication with the crew in the forward torpedo room of the *Squalus*. Then the bow of the *Sculpin* surged up on a wave and the buoy cable and telephone line parted.

By 1245 the Navy Department had been informed of the *Squalus* disaster and immediately one of the biggest submarine rescue and salvage operations in naval history began to unfold. Divers and salvage personnel and crews of salvage ships and tugs were recalled to their vessels. The ASR (submarine rescue vessel) *Falcon* got steam up and headed toward the sunken *Squalus* under forced draft. On deck was the McCann submarine rescue bell that had been developed after the S-4 disaster in 1927. Commander McCann was on board to be in charge of bell rescue, if this was required. Lieutenant Commander Momsen was detailed to the rescue to supervise escape via the escape lungs which he had developed, if this was the chosen method of rescue. Lieutenant Behnke, Navy medical officer and dive accident specialist was also on board. Fourteen divers and a diving officer had arrived from Newport just as the *Falcon* was leaving the dock. These 14 divers, plus 7 in the ship's company, would be the initial diving team. The tug *Penacook*, with Admiral Cole aboard, left Portsmouth for the one hour run to the site of the sinking. The large tug *Wandank* was next to reach the scene. She used her oscillators to try to communicate with the *Squalus* while the *Penacook* began dragging a heavy grapnel that eventually hooked onto the sub. During the night the rescue fleet continued to grow: a cruiser, two Coast Guard patrol boats, the tug *Chandler*, and, at daybreak, a patrol plane that circled overhead to try to spot any of the crew who might escape from the *Squalus* with Momsen lungs.

Before dawn on May 24, the rescue vessel *Falcon* arrived with the divers and the rescue chamber on board. The commanding officer, Lieutenant George Sharp, worked in dark, stormy conditions to lay a six anchor, chain and buoy mooring system that would securely hold the rescue vessel directly over the sunken *Squalus*. By 0646 the rescue vessel completed her moor. Twenty-two hours had passed since the *Squalus* had touched on the bottom.

In the *Squalus*, cold was beginning to affect the crew. Temperature inside the vessel was already down to 46°F. Men who had been in the water as they escaped from the after engine room into the control room—Isaacs, Blanchard, Mannes, and O'Hara—were suffering most from the intense cold. Lieutenant Naquin gathered up all the blankets available, and gave one of the men his own jacket for warmth. All were listening intently—and apprehensively—to the sounds of the rescue ship and gear working over their sunken boat.

On board the *Falcon* conventional surface supplied helmet dive gear was being rigged. The *Falcon* was also supplied complete sets of dive equipment for using the recently developed mix of oxygen and helium as a breathing gas. However, while this mix had been used experimentally several times by many of the rescue divers no diver had ever used it under the conditions of depth, cold and urgency now facing the salvage and rescue personnel. The divers, and rescue officials, felt it was better to go with equipment and breathing gas they knew the most about.

While the diving gear was being readied for the first dive to the *Squalus* other crew members were rigging the McCann submarine rescue bell. This is a steel device about 11 feet tall and weighing 18,000 pounds. It has a maximum outside diameter of nearly eight feet, tapering at the bottom to five feet. The bottom of the bell is open and, in a groove, has a rubber gasket which seals on a skirt around the escape hatch of the submarine. The chamber is divided into three compartments; the upper or control compartment, the lower compartment, and the ballast tanks. Necessary fittings and connections are found on the top outside hull for air supply and vent hoses, electrical wiring and telephone cables. A hatch in the top permits entry and exit of the operators and rescued personnel. Between the upper and lower compartments a second hatch permits access into the lower, open end of the bell and thus into or out of the sunken submarine when the bell is mated to the escape hatch. All operating valves and fittings are in the upper compartment of the chamber. An air driven motor pulls the bell down to the submarine by reeling in a wire previously attached to the submarine escape hatch bail by a diver. Usually the chamber operates at atmospheric pressure since the internal compartment of a submarine from which the crew is to be rescued will also be at atmospheric pressure, or nearly so.

By 1010 Martin Conrad Sibitzky had been dressed in his 200 pounds of air-supplied helmet gear. He was a good choice for this difficult dive. He was young, tough, and experienced. He had made many practice dives in connection with hooking up the rescue bell and knew just what he had to do. But, he had never made a working dive in 242 feet of cold water before.

At 1012 he was hoisted over the side of the *Falcon* into the water and worked his way forward to the cable leading up from the grapnel snagged on the *Squalus*. He checked his gear and left the surface. At 1017, his heavy shoes landed with the dull thud of lead on steel. Sibitzky knew he was on the deck of the *Squalus*. But where?

Visibility was much better than anyone thought it would be. He could see 30 to 40 feet in all directions. He needed good visibility. Cold numbed his touch, and narcosis his thinking, and so much depended on his observations and reports to topside salvage and rescue personnel.

Sibitzky turned slowly around, mentally absorbing everything within sight. In the slurred voice of a man at great depth on air he reported, "I've landed on the submarine," he told his talker topside, "I am on the bow of the *Squalus*." Then he leaned over to look at an object on deck. "I am looking at the forward anchor winch." Now he turned to face aft. The grapnel had snagged just six feet from the torpedo room escape hatch through which the trapped submariners must escape. He reported this to the surface and asked them to send him the rescue bell downhaul cable. Sibitzky stamped his lead soled shoes on the deck to let the crew of the *Squalus* know he was there. Answering bangs on the hull with a hammer told him some of the crew were alive and just a thin metal hull away from him. He got some slack in the down haul cable, unscrewed the shackle pin, placed the open end over the bail of the escape hatch and replaced the shackle pin, securing it with a safety wire to prevent loss. Over the telephone he reported, "Job completed." He received three pulls on his lifeline telling him to stand by to come up and, when he answered, four pulls told him he was going to be pulled up. His feet cleared the deck of the *Squalus* at 1039, he reached the surface at 1124 and was placed in the recompression chamber for further decompression.

The McCann rescue bell was ready. At 1130 the chamber was hoisted over the side. Bell operators John Mihalowski and Walter Harmon boarded the chamber and at 1159 began the first trip down.

The chamber reached the *Squalus* at 1212 and was settled easily on the rubber gasket around the hatch. Now came a critical part of the operation. First, Mihalowski and Harmon had to blow the lower compartment of the bell dry; then vent it so both compartments of the bell were at atmospheric pressure. If this were done properly the force of 242 feet of water would hold the

Lowered from the vessel Falcon, *the McCann rescue bell is mated to the* Squalus' *escape hatch 242 feet underwater. The first of seven men were rescued from the sub 28 hours after it sank. The rescue of all 33* Squalus *survivors took four trips by the McCann bell. Painting by Bill Hamilton.*

rescue bell to the escape hatch of the submarine. Mihalowski, who was operating the chamber, watched the lower compartment through the small glass port in the hatch. When it appeared this was dry he vented the pressure. He opened the hatch and dropped quickly into the lower compartment. But, instead of being dry it still had eight inches of icy water. Mihalowski recoiled from the cold but fastened the four safety bolts from the deck of the *Squalus* to slots in the lower edge of the chamber. When he was finished, Mihalowski was wet and shivering. He unhooked the downhaul wire, moved it aside, turned the wheel of the submarine hatch very slowly and, when he heard a slight hissing of escaping air, he knew rescue was possible. The small amount of water in the lower compartment of the bell dropped into the sub. Then the flood light in the bottom of the rescue bell lit up the face of Lieutenant (jg) J. C. Nichols, the first man ever to be rescued from a sunken submarine. It was 1245. Just 28 hours had passed since the *Squalus* had touched bottom.

Inside the submarine Lt. Naquin had ordered Lt. Nichols to be the first man out of the boat. He wanted at least one responsible person to reach the surface in case something happened and the rest of the crew could not be rescued. Then those men who appeared in the worst physical condition were ordered into the bell. By 1315 the transfer of seven survivors was completed. During the transfer, Mihalowski passed down blankets, hot soup and coffee, and sandwiches. With the bell's air system he blew fresh air into the submarine. At 1342 the bell reached the surface and discharged the first seven survivors.

Ten minutes later the bell started to the bottom for a second load. Operators of the rescue bell were W. E. Harmon and W. Badders. Mihalowski was below deck on the *Falcon* getting into dry clothes. At 1441 the rescue bell reached the deck of the sub for a second time. At 1515 the bell was secured and the hatch opened to receive nine more survivors.

By 1624 the rescue bell was ready for the third trip; operators—Mihalowski and Badders. There was some minor trouble engaging the clutch of the air motor that was to pull them down. But by 1702 they had reached the sub and by 1801 nine more survivors were aboard and ready for ascent. At 1827 the bell reached the surface again.

The chamber started down on the fourth and last trip to the forward escape hatch at 1841; operators—Mihalowski and McDonald. By 1931 they had reached the *Squalus* and at 1941 opened the hatch and took seven passengers on board. Lt. Naquin was the last to leave the *Squalus*. At 2011 the chamber started toward the surface, but 11 minutes later, at 200 feet, the bell stalled. The winch would not work. Mihalowski tried to bring the bell up on the brake but at 155 feet this too, failed and the chamber sank to 210 feet. Mihalowski looked out the port in the side of the chamber and could see the conning tower of the *Squalus*.

A suspenseful hour passed while topside personnel tried to make a decision on how to get the bell back to the surface. Finally, at 2112, diver W. H. Squire left the surface to cut the bell downhaul cable loose from the *Squalus*. This was done and Squire left the bottom at 2123.

The crew of the *Falcon* then started hoisting the rescue bell toward the surface. At 200 feet the chamber stopped and then suddenly lowered to the bottom where it landed alongside the *Squalus*.

It had been decided topside that a diver should be sent down to the rescue bell to attach a new lifting cable to the top of it. At 2149 diver J. E. Duncan left the surface. During his descent he

Operator of the McCann rescue bell, John Mihalowski (left), and E.R. Cross. Photo courtesy Myrtice Squire.

noticed the lifting cable on the bell was frayed so badly only a few strands of wire were holding its weight. At 2155 he reached the rescue bell, but his reports became incoherent and faint. He was hoisted to the surface and placed in the recompression chamber. In the rescue bell the personnel were in no great danger. Fresh air could be maintained and they had good communication with the surface. The great hazard was from the cold; the temperature in the chamber continued to fall. By 2245 a second diver, E. P. Clayton, left the surface to secure the new lifting cable to the chamber. He experienced trouble with the dive lights (it was now night) and his air hose continued to foul in the cables, hoses, and ropes. Again at a depth of 232 feet the diver became confused and had to be pulled to the surface.

At four minutes past midnight, May 25, 1939, it was decided to blow ballast from the rescue bell until it became light enough to be lifted by hand. If too much ballast water was blown from the bell it would float violently to the surface with disastrous results. If too little, the bell would be too heavy for the crew to lift by hand. In the chamber Mihalowski carefully blew ballast until the bell barely had negative buoyancy. Then the crew of the *Falcon*, with cold, bare hands, pulled on the frayed wire until the bell reached the surface. At 0023, nearly five hours after it left the bottom, the last seven of the 32 were discharged from the bell.

By 1341 on May 25, the crew of the *Falcon* had rested and personnel were being readied for dives to the after rescue hatch of the *Squalus*. In the next three hours three dives were made to the after deck to connect the bell downhaul cable. Two of the divers became totally disoriented and confused and one of these lapsed into unconsciousness. The third diver, while adversely affected by nitrogen narcosis, was able with difficulty to perform the simple task of shackling a wire to the bail of the escape hatch.

Mihalowski and Badders had secured the rescue chamber over the after escape hatch of the *Squalus* at 1803. The pressure in the bell was, in this case, increased until equal to the surrounding water pressure. The lower hatch was opened and, according to Badders, as he turned the wheel that unlocked the escape hatch, it began to shake and vibrate as a blast of air poured out of the submarine escape hatch into the bell. Badders tried quickly to close and refasten the hatch but before this could be done he was waist deep in ice cold water in the lower compartment of the bell. In the upper compartment, Mihalowski quickly blew high pressure air into the lower chamber. This stopped the inrush of water and then forced the water back into the *Squalus*. Badders then slowly opened the hatch of the sub and he and Mihalowski reported they saw only oily, black water. The submarine escape hatch and the lower hatch of the bell were closed and dogged down tight and the chamber started for the surface. The rescue phase of the *Squalus* disaster was over.

On May 26, 1939, the tremendous job of salvaging the *Squalus* began. One hundred and thirteen days later the vessel was in drydock, one day before her first birthday. More than 50 divers made a total of 640 dives during the operation.

E.R. CROSS

Salvage of the Squalus

On May 23, 1939, the United States submarine USS *Squalus* sank off Portsmouth, New Hampshire, with all hands. But 32 of the crew plus one civilian worker were rescued the next day. One hundred thirteen days after the disaster the *Squalus* was in drydock. It had been raised from 242 feet by the valiant efforts of 53 divers. They risked their lives making 640 dives during the desperate, frustrating work. For the sixth and last time, the *Squalus* had been raised.

This is the story of the 113 days; of the first use of oxygen-helium for deep diving in the open sea; of blow-ups from 240 feet of water; of bends cases and accidents; of the terrible danger to men working to rig pontoons weighing 35 tons each in strong currents and heavy surge; of the striking success of some divers and the stark failure of others; and of anxiety, euphoria, and unconsciousness caused by nitrogen narcosis.

The Squalus

In May 1939, the USS *Squalus* (pronounced "skwaylus") was one of the U.S. Navy's newest S-type submarines. She was 310 feet long and displaced some 1,450 tons on the surface and 2,000 tons when submerged. She could cruise on the surface at 16 knots. Except for one test run the boat had completed her builders' trials. That last test run was to be a crash dive from the surface—cruising at 16 knots—to a depth of 50 feet in only 60 seconds. The order, "Take her down," was given by Commanding Officer, Lieutenant Oliver Naquin, at 0840 on May 23, 1939. Within five minutes, the *Squalus* rested on the bottom in 242 feet of water with her three after compartments flooded and 26 of her crew dead. The forward two compartments were not flooded and 32 men were rescued during the next 40 hours.

The last man was rescued from the *Squalus* a few minutes past midnight on May 25, 1939. According to a Naval officer, "We have finished lifesaving and our task has turned to that of salvage."

The Salvors

A fleet of watercraft of all sizes had gathered over the stricken submarine. The key vessel was the submarine rescue and salvage ship USS *Falcon*, Lieutenant George Sharp commanding. The *Falcon* was an ex-minesweeper first commissioned in 1918 during WW I. Later converted to a submarine rescue and salvage ship, she had been used to raise the USS *S-51* sunk off Block Island in 132 feet of water in September 1925 and in recovering the USS *S-4* from 104 feet of water in December 1927. The *Falcon* and her crew were not strangers to submarine disasters.

On this operation the *Falcon* would serve a dual work role. Primarily she would be a diving platform. She would also provide hyperbaric facilities for surface decompression procedures and for treatment of diver diseases or accidents.

The sister submarine USS *Sculpin* was there, too. The crew

of this vessel had located the sunken *Squalus* and would now provide reserve air and other support. She was also a valuable reference for those diving on the *Squalus*. Since they were identical vessels, the divers could locate on the *Sculpin* the fittings, valves, compartments, etc., they were going to work with on the *Squalus*. The *Sculpin* also served as flagship for Admiral Syrus Cole, commander of the salvage force.

Some of the Navy's top diving and submarine experts were at the scene: Lieutenant Commander F. A. Tusler was the salvage officer. Also, Lieutenant Commander Momsen, who had developed the Momsen submarine escape lung; Commanders A. I. McKee and A. R. McCann, developers of the submarine rescue bell; Navy diving medical specialists doctors Behnke, Yarborough, and Willmon. And, there were the hundreds of enlisted men and 53 divers.

The Divers

A total of 53 divers worked on the rescue of the sub crew and on a job that is referred to as one of the greatest salvage efforts of all time.

Navy divers are, invariably, tough, healthy, easygoing when not diving, psychologically well adjusted and liked by the rest of the world. But working at a depth of 240 feet put physiological and psychological stress on them they had never before experienced. The extremely cold water, currents, darkness, the weather and, frequently, lack of proper equipment and the use of new, untried equipment, caused further stress. Not one of all the divers was able to complete all of the objectives of his dives. In spite of this the salvors scored a striking success in raising the sub.

The Salvage Plan

The plan finally approved for the salvage involved techniques
and equipment first used to raise the submarine *F-4* sunk off
Honolulu in 306 feet of water in March 1915. Some refinements
were made in both equipment and techniques in the later salvage
of the *S-51* in 1925 and the *S-4* in 1927.

Basically, the plan involved placing heavy chains and lifting
slings under the hull in both the bow and stern sections of the
boat. The salvage pontoons, themselves small vessels, were 32
feet long, 12.5 feet in diameter and weighed 35 tons. Each was
capable of lifting 115 tons (80 tons net lift). They would be rigged
to the lifting chains—six over the flooded stern, four over the
bow for the first lift. In addition, some of the compartments on
the *Squalus* could be blown dry to obtain additional buoyancy.

In order to prevent an uncontrolled blow-up of the sub from
deep water, it was to be raised in three stages. First, from the
depth of 242 to about 160 feet; then to a depth of about 90; and
finally to a depth that would permit drydocking. At the 90 foot
depth divers could work long enough to close hatches and
prepare the submarine for final tow into the harbor and
drydocking.

Day 1: May 26

The first day of salvage started early. *Falcon* was shifted from her
mooring used for the rescue work until she was in a better
position for the salvage work. By 1130 the new moor was
completed. At 1136 diver J. J. Alicki went over the side and at
1140 reported he was on the deck of the *Squalus*. Diver F. E.

The USS Sculpin *assisted in the salvage of her sister sub, USS* Squalus.
Photo courtesy Myrtice Squire.

Smith left the surface at 1141 and landed on the vessel at 1144.
Both men used compressed air and standard Navy MK-V helmet
diving gear. Their job was simple—attach a four inch diameter
Manila line to the rail of the sub that would be used as a descent
and ascent line by the divers.

Alicki reported he was unable to drag the heavy line forward
and had gone back to see why Smith was not feeding him slack.
He stated, "Smith was sitting on deck with his back to the rail. I
let the rope go, checked Smith's control valve to see if he was
getting air. Then I jerked him a few times and tried to talk to
him." Alicki reported he felt very tired while on the bottom.
Smith states, "I landed on the deck of the sub and was waiting for
the line to come down. My next recollection was of awakening
from a deep sleep. I must have passed out instantly as I have no
recollection of going to sleep. I had no bad feelings before or
after."

The next dive was to a depth of only 102 feet to clear some
wires that had become fouled. The time of the dive was 15

minutes and it was completed without incident. Then O. L. (bo's'n) Crandall made a dive on compressed air to the deck of the submarine. He left the surface at 1524. At 1529 Crandall reported he was on the sub. Two minutes later his speech became incoherent and rambling. He was ordered to come up and was on the decompression stage at 1536. There had been four dives and three failures. Nitrogen narcosis had exacted its toll.

It was thought the ship's diving air supply might not be properly filtered for such deep diving. Lieutenant Willmon, a diving physiologist, and William Badders started a dry dive to 300 feet on air in the recompression chamber to test the air supply. At a depth of 210 feet the air supply was exhausted. They had to surface.

Day one was over. It seemed to presage the way the salvage job would go during the next 112 days.

Use of Heliox

Experimental work with heliox (helium oxygen) diving began with the Navy in 1924 and continued through 1940. In the later stages it was at the Navy's Experimental Diving Unit. By 1943 wet dives to 500 feet in experimental dive tanks and open sea dives to 440 feet had been made. In 1937 Max Gene Nohl made a test dive to 420 feet in Lake Michigan. Contrary to expectations, the use of heliox mixes did not permit material reduction in decompression time. However, it allowed much deeper dives to be made with greater safety.

Several divers who had been rushed to the *Squalus* salvage had been stationed at the U.S. Navy Experimental Diving Unit at Washington, D.C. They had been working on developing and testing heliox for diving. However, this mixture had only been used experimentally under carefully controlled conditions.

In conventional air-supplied helmets, air freeflows constantly into and out of the helmet. Part is inhaled and then exhaled by the diver but there is no recirculation or reuse of any of the air. In the heliox mode a diving helmet has additional valves, a venturi system for recirculating the mixed gas from the helmet through a carbon dioxide absorbing canister and chemical. While the gas supply is still basically in a constant flow state, the volume of gas actually needed by the diver is small when compared with a conventional air supply system.

The 1943 *U.S. Navy Diving Manual* states, "Oxygen helium mixtures were used almost entirely by the divers in the salvage of the USS *Squalus.* . . ." It is true, heliox mixes were used to some extent during the salvage but not nearly as much, and not with as much success, as almost all writers have indicated.

Day 2: May 27

On this day the first field trial of the Navy's heliox diving rig was made by F. H. O'Keefe. His dive started at 1006. He descended to 50 feet for 15 minutes. The item of note in the log was that his nose was skinned by the tenders when they put his helmet over his head.

Later on day two, at 1130, R. M. Metzger made a test dive with the heliox rig to 100 feet. Everything worked well. Metzger stated, "I felt normal at all times. No aftereffects."

At 1255 the first working dive ever with a heliox rig was attempted by William (Bill) Badders, an excellent choice for this test of man and equipment in deep water. He was dressed in the special helmet. He landed on the sub at 1308 and reported he was near the deck gun just aft the conning tower. He tried to drag the four inch descending line into position. According to Badders, "As I reached the gun the recirculator on the helmet seemed to gradually be losing gas supply. I opened the main control valve and the recirculating venturi tube seemed to start functioning properly again for about one minute, then started to slow down again. I felt as though I were being overcome with CO_2. I made sure I was clear and notified topside to start bringing me up immediately. As I approached the surface my physical well being improved. I was then brought to the surface for decompression."

At 1511 A. W. Pickering made a 240 foot dive on compressed air. He was able to secure the descending line to the sub. He completed the job in nine minutes and surfaced with no ill effects. Badders and Pickering were out of the decompression chamber at 1634.

So ended day two. One line had been attached to the sunken sub.

The third and fourth uses of heliox diving systems were made on day three. Zampiglione and Gilbert descended to the submarine. Zampiglione reported no problems during a 33 minute dive. Gilbert reported that the breathing gas seemed to be shutting off at irregular intervals. Also, the main control valve failed to deliver adequate gas and his dive was aborted.

On day four Bill Badders and A. J. Vanderhayden made dives on compressed air to 240 feet. Air rushing into Badders' helmet, effects of nitrogen narcosis, and the poor quality of the telephone system available made good communication impossible and the dive was terminated. Vanderhayden reported, "The dive was normal in all respects and I felt good at all times." In use at that time was the Pittsburgh sound powered telephone.

Day 5: May 30

One diver reported: "Telephone reception very poor. Turned my air down to hear. From then on I felt kind of woozy. Before I could get back to normal, I was hoisted up." A second diver stated, "After reaching the submarine I waited a minute or two before attempting any work as my head was not exactly clear." Later this diver opened his helmet exhaust fully and increased the flow of air through his helmet. He said, "After that my head cleared up quickly." Martin Sibitzky, who made the first dive on the *Squalus* to hook up the rescue bell, was the third diver down that day. He related, "I was slightly dizzy on the bottom and became very dizzy when I cut down my air to listen to the telephone. I am sure I was conscious all of the time." Two more divers, Baker and Lieutenant Morrison, made dives using compressed air on day five. Both reported using "plenty of air" and were able to complete their tasks.

Day 6: May 31

At 0726 John Mihalowski, who had made four trips with the bell to rescue personnel from the submarine, made a dive using the heliox diving system with a new rack arrangement. He stated, "When I landed on the submarine I was breathing heavily for about 30 seconds. I could feel the water on my arms. It was bitterly cold. I was cold from the time I left the surface. I started to feel sort of lightheaded and thought I had better come up, so I came up. While I was on the decompression stage the gas supply came in an irregular flow."

Seven more dives were made that day and each of the divers

completed his assigned tasks. All used compressed air. E. P. Clayton became fouled in his air hose slack, but was able to clear himself and make a normal ascent.

Day 7: June 1

On this day, off the English coast, the British submarine *Thetis* sank with a loss of 99 lives. Like the *Squalus*, she was on her initial sea trials.

Seven dives were made on the *Squalus* on day seven, all using compressed air. One diver stated, "I was knocked off the descending line, fell about 15 feet and landed in the mud beside the submarine. I climbed back on the boat but was unable to loosen the shackle pin." He was brought up after a 25 minute dive. A second diver stated, "While trying to cut a line loose I dropped my knife. After I found it I felt dizzy. When I increased my air supply I got worse." He was brought to the surface after six minutes.

Five dives were completed without incident and all jobs were accomplished. However, it was obvious that working dives to 240 feet were going to present problems. With compressed air the major difficulty seemed to be the effects of nitrogen narcosis. It is known that a build-up of CO_2 in the breathing gas will intensify the effect of nitrogen under pressure. The use of lots of air during the dive helped most divers with the problem but did not eliminate the potential hazards completely. The use of excess air for helmet circulation also increased the possibility of an uncontrolled blow-up from depth.

The use of the basically untried heliox dive helmet and gas system also resulted in problems. The venturi system continued to fail intermittently. This was probably owing to icing of the system that blocked, or partially blocked, the venturi system that recirculated the breathing gas mixture from the CO_2 absorbent canister back into the helmet. Again, a CO_2 build-up, even when using helium, caused problems.

A known factor of using helium mix as the breathing gas is that helium will transfer heat from the body many times faster than compressed air. Because of this the divers using heliox mixes suffered intense cold. Of the 14 dives made on days six and seven, 13 of them used compressed air and were basically uneventful. The dive made using heliox resulted in the diver becoming dangerously cold.

Day 8: June 2

Early on day eight Lieutenant Laing made a dive to 240 feet using a heliox gas mix with a standard air helmet; a straight, open circulation gas supply with no CO_2 scrubbing. He also used another "shocking" first—electrically heated underwear. His statements are revealing. "The dive was a very easy one with no mental disturbance. My faculties were clear at all times." Later in his report he said, "I did experience some communication difficulties due to the fact that I had the hood of the electrically heated underwear over my ears and it was also due to the fact that the lead wire to the underwear worked around between my mouth and the telephone transceiver." Still later in the dive the lieutenant recalled, "Coming up my hands got pretty cold. I called for more heat, which I felt around my body, but which I did not appreciably feel on my hands."

Power for the electrically heated underwear was from a

direct current source, either from appropriate battery supply or from some other DC source. Current supply, and therefore the amount of heat to the diver's underwear, was controlled by adding or taking away batteries, or by a system of resistors. Neither system was very accurate, responsive, or reliable. There were also cases of mild, but harmless, shock when wires became bare or the suit got wet for any of several reasons. While not hazardous the occasional shocks were a definite distraction for the diver already affected by depth.

In addition to the equipment problems and the effects of the breathing gases, the lack of experience of the divers in working at 240 feet on a sunken submarine posed problems in the first several days of the operation. The divers' physical condition also played a part since they were not able to cope, in many cases, with the extreme exertion needed. All too often, conditions similar to the one reported by a diver on day 9 occurred: "I missed the submarine and landed on the bottom; got fouled in the hose around the bottom. The exertion caused by working to clear myself tired me out completely and I had to be brought to the surface."

In spite of all the problems, the work continued. The plans called for reinforced hoses to be connected to control room air salvage fittings, forward battery, and forward torpedo rooms. Also, lifting slings were to be swept under the bow of the boat. By May 31 this was done.

During June, more air hoses were connected to the several main ballast tanks. Discharge hoses were connected to the sub's port and starboard fuel oil (diesel) tanks (two on each side). Recovering the fuel from the *Squalus* proved to be quite simple. Water hoses were led from each fuel tank into an empty tank on the salvage vessel. When sea water flooded the sub's fuel tanks, the diesel fuel "floated" up the hoses and into the salvage vessel's tanks. The tanks on the sub could then be blown dry and used for flotation without creating an environmental problem and a potentially hazardous fuel spill.

Also started in June was an attempt to reeve lifting slings under the stern of the sub by the use of a special water jet lance. The original lance proved unsatisfactory. It was impossible to retain correct alignment and the diver had difficulty making up the sections of the lance while at depth in cold water. Working with the tunneling hoses started on day 10 and the final tunnel was not completed until day 28 (June 22). In the meantime a new lance was designed and constructed.

A seven inch diameter Manila tow line was rigged to the stern of the submarine on June 29. It seemed the salvage work was progressing nicely, but this was day 35. Counting the two days of rescue, the divers had been working for 33 days with only two days off. Even these days were not for relaxation. The entire crew was tired and every task was an accident about to happen. There were several cases of dizziness in the divers; one was knocked off the descending line and fell the rest of the way to the ocean bottom; two missed the decompression stage on the way to the surface and had to descend quickly to the proper depth for the first in-water decompression stop at 80 feet. A warrant officer made one dive to 240 feet, surfaced after six minutes and asked to be transferred.

Day 16: June 10

This was a day of near disaster for two divers. O. S. Payne reached the submarine. He stated, "I started getting dizzy so I stopped to turn on more air to clear my head. The next thing I knew I had been hauled to the surface." His tenders reported he had blown to the surface (made an uncontrolled ascent) owing to excess air in his suit.

W. H. Squire, an experienced master diver, was working in 240 feet of water using a heliox mix. He reported, "I returned to the descending line and was standing by to come up and that was the end as far as I remember." But there was more, much more, to the story than that. A news article states, "Squire had made a routine dive when he suddenly shot to the surface alongside the salvage ship *Falcon*. His diving suit, blown up like a toy balloon, was tangled in life lines, air hoses, and descending ropes. Squire floated helplessly on the surface while two divers jumped fully clothed into the sea to untangle the diver and pull him to the side of the ship." Squire suffered an attack of the bends, the first on the job, and had to spend ten hours in the recompression chamber.

In spite of all this, the job was progressing. Diving usually started about 0730. Dives to 240 feet lasted 15 to 20 minutes. The last diver was generally brought on board and placed in the chamber at about 1830 for the 60 minutes of required surface decompression.

Decompression procedures followed for heliox diving were for the diver to take his first decompression stop at 80 or 90 feet. He was then brought to the surface and placed in the recompression chamber where the first decompression stop was repeated. This was followed by the balance of the prescribed decompression for the particular dive, usually about 90 minutes. Sometimes suits were torn and divers got wet with freezing water. Never was a dive a "comfortable" one. Perhaps this job is where the saying originated, "You never ask a diver how he feels. Just ask him where he hurts."

Day 22: June 16

On this day there was a third operational submarine disaster. The French submarine *Phenix*, with her crew of 71, was lost in 300 feet of water.

Day 37: July 1

Air hoses were now rigged to the various compartments and tanks of the submarine. Preparations were started to rig and place the huge salvage pontoons that had been brought to the job. Some of them were 32 feet long by 12.5 feet in diameter and had a lifting capacity of 115 tons and a weight of 35 tons. This gave a net lift of 80 tons for each pontoon. Each was divided into three compartments and had blow and vent controls. Hawse pipes were installed in each of the two end compartments through which two and a half inch diameter chains and lifting slings were fitted. At the prescribed depth, a stopper called a "flower pot"—because of its shape—was used. Each of these devices weighed 800 pounds and had to be locked in place by the divers. One end of each pontoon was painted white; the other end red so divers could determine which end needed to be adjusted. On a turning, unpainted pontoon, both ends look the same.

The theory was that the sub would be lightened by blowing water from the various compartments until a negative buoyancy was reached that could be overcome by the pontoons. This would prevent an uncontrolled ascent (with probably disastrous results) since, once the uppermost pontoons reached the surface, the ascent would stop.

Day 40: July 4

At 1831, R. M. Metzger made a dive to one of the salvage pontoons. His report: "Landed on the pontoon. Went to the white end, saw the flower pot was in place. Hammered wedges in the flower pot. Did the same thing to the red end. Came up. The pontoon was level." Metzger was out of the decompression chamber at 1946. It had been a typically long day. News headlines ashore stated, "Pontoons in place to lift *Squalus*." But were they?

Day 44: July 8

Martin Sibitzky made a dive on YSP-31 (YSP stands for Yard Salvage Pontoon). Sibitzky reported, "Landed on white end of pontoon. It was at an angle of about 30 degrees. Was instructed to open the vent valve, which I did. Then came up."

Day 49: July 13

Five more hard working days had passed. Day 49 came in with gusty winds and rough seas. But F. E. Smith made a dive at 0602 to attach an air hose to the number two main ballast tank. He also opened the blow valve and closed the submarine's control room salvage air valve. How could the divers work and find what they were supposed to? There was now a staggering total of 28,000 feet of ropes, wires, chains, and miscellaneous "things" over the side of the *Falcon* and connected to the *Squalus* or to the seven pontoons now rigged in a manner that, it was hoped, would raise the boat. A Portsmouth, New Hampshire paper reported, "Salvage ship blowing air into pontoons on *Squalus*."

The *Falcon* had three separate supplies of compressed air. There were two large compressors capable of supplying 150 cubic feet of air per minute at a pressure of 400 psi for the helmet divers. For salvage, two compressors delivered very high volumes of air at 150 psi. Emergency air was stored in large banks of compressed air cylinders. In addition, a large diameter air hose (actually a two and a half inch fire hose being used as an air hose) ran from *Sculpin* to provide additional air to the salvage manifold. From the manifold, called the "calliope" by the divers, ran dozens of air hoses leading to the many pontoons and submarine fittings far below the surface.

By 0913 compressed air was rapidly displacing the water in both the *Squalus* and the pontoons. Bubbles were boiling to the surface. Pontoons attached to the stern of the sub came up first under perfect control. First one salvage pontoon and then a second surfaced at the bow. Only one of them was supposed to come completely to the surface. Something was wrong. Moments later the bow of the sunken sub roared out of the water. Very shortly, more than 20 feet of the 1,500 ton boat was above the surface. Headlines ashore told the story: "*Squalus* shoots to surface, sinks again; 21 divers periled as craft whips the sea."

The next day a Portsmouth newspaper headlined, "Heavy seas prevent divers from learning *Squalus* damage." Divers were again working underwater by day 52, July 16. The seven pontoons the divers had spent months rigging were tangled with ropes, hoses and chains but were still in place. The divers had done their work well. For five more days, the divers and the salvage crew had to strip away literally miles of wire, hoses and chains to untangle the mess left when the submarine surfaced violently and sank back to the bottom.

During the first attempt to raise her the Squalus *roared to the surface then sank back into 242 feet of water. Photo courtesy Myrtice Squire.*

Day 71: August 4

One of the most serious accidents occurred on day 71. E. B. Crosby made a dive to 240 feet using heliox. After 17 minutes he was brought toward the surface. He was given the first three decompression stops in the water at depths of 80, 60, and 50 feet, then transferred to the chamber for surface decompression procedures. While being recompressed at about the 50 foot level, he developed a severe pain in his abdomen. The recompression was continued at 130 feet. He responded to treatment and was decompressed to surface pressure over the next three hours. Crosby remained in good condition until about 1800 when he became nauseated and had serious vision problems. He was again placed in the chamber and recompressed to 200 feet. After 20 minutes at depth, his vision was normal and decompression was started again. Crosby's treatment was completed at 1030 on August 6. He was transferred to a hospital on shore for observation. Crosby was back on board the salvage vessel and diving again on August 27 and continued to dive until September 9.

During Crosby's treatment there was no diving since the chamber was not available for surface decompression or for an emergency.

On August 8, a sudden, violent thunderstorm with 50 mile per hour winds whipped the sea, delaying the attempt to raise the *Squalus*. But on August 12, newspapers told the story, "The sunken submarine was lifted 76 feet today and rested on an even keel." After divers had inspected pontoons, air hoses, and fittings, the *Squalus* was towed at a speed of one knot toward shore until she again grounded at a depth of 172 feet.

At this shallower depth divers could work longer periods. Rerigging the pontoons went faster now; partly because of the shallower water but also owing to the divers' having a great deal more experience with handling the equipment. Heliox was still used for many of the dives.

Day 80: August 13

It was Sunday and there was no diving on this day. President Roosevelt visited the salvage job.

Day 84: August 17

All was ready and Admiral Cole opted to make the second lift. Again, thousands of feet of hoses were put into service and the water was forced out of the compartments of the sub and the salvage pontoons. The *Squalus* slowly floated to a preplanned depth of 92 feet. There were no problems and the sub was towed to a shallow area where it was temporarily grounded while the salvage crew made ready for the next lift.

For the next 29 days the salvage crew and divers worked long hours clearing the sub of lines, chains, and hoses and rerigging pontoons, salvage hoses, and tow lines for the final lift and the tow into the harbor and drydock. Now, at a depth of only 92 feet, the divers could work more hours each day. However, fog, turbidity, heavy swells, and ocean currents made jobs even more difficult and hazardous. Thirty-five ton pontoons whipping back and forth in heavy ocean surges were things to be careful about.

Day 90: August 23

Martin Sibitzky performed another first. He reported, "Took pictures of Porter (another diver working on the sub with him) and of the submarine as directed. Completed other assigned tasks. Surfaced." This is the only reference to underwater photography noted in all the reports on the salvage of the *Squalus*.

Day 93: August 26

William Squire and Henry Frye made a dive and reported, "Working together we took off the main engine induction valve cover plate, took off the cap, screwed the valve down 43 turns." Finally, the valve that had failed to close on May 23, causing the *Squalus* to sink, was closed to the Atlantic Ocean.

Day 95: August 28

The British submarine *Thetis* was raised this day and towed to drydock where her 99 dead were removed.

The *Squalus* was ready for what was hoped would be the last lift. High pressure air roared into the two pontoons and into the hull of the sub. The bow came to the surface first. But the vessel listed heavily to starboard, spilled out the air, and sank again.

Later that day another attempt was made to float the sub. The stern was blown dry with compressed air. All the water in the hull rushed to the forward part of the vessel and the sub sank.

Two weeks of intermittent squally weather and rough seas followed. Divers and salvage crews fought the elements.

On shore, newspapers told part of the story, "September 2: Naval officials announced tonight that a pontoon had knocked off an after torpedo room hatch during the storm this week. A new hatch and a buffer to protect it would have to be installed." The following day Duncan and Crosby (the diver who had suffered the serious case of the bends) made a dive on the sub. Crosby reported, "Duncan and I hauled the new hatch cover that was sent down over to the hatch and secured it." The dive lasted 40 minutes.

Pontoons had also been damaged during the storm and had to be replaced.

Day 100: September 2

Diver Metzger suffered a bends hit in his left arm. He was treated and there were no residual symptoms. He returned to duty and made one more dive on September 9.

From September 9-12 heavy seas hampered the final place-

The fourth time she was raised, this time from only 92 feet of water, the Squalus *had a pronounced starboard list and sank to the bottom again. Photo courtesy Myrtice Squire.*

ment and rigging for lifting and towing the *Squalus.* Headlines in Portsmouth papers told the story. "September 11. Last *Squalus* lift due tomorrow." Then, "September 12. *Squalus* final lift slated tomorrow." And again, "September 13. *Squalus* lifted, but sinks again." This was a report as of 0955. Later that day the *Squalus* was again floated to the surface. This time she was nearly on an even keel and the slow tow to Portsmouth and drydock began.

Day 112: September 14

"Delay again dogs *Squalus* salvage crew:" Such was a headline in a Portsmouth paper after the sub was docked temporarily. "The stern of the submarine, berthed at the Navy Yard pier, sank below the surface."

The sea was still reluctant to give up its dead. Later that night the salvage crew finally won out against her. The stern was raised and the vessel put on an almost even keel. A few minutes before midnight the doomed shipmates were removed from the vessel.

The *Squalus* was drydocked the next day—September 15, 1939; 113 days after it sank. The vessel was exactly one year old. President Roosevelt formally commended the "devotion to duty, courage, skill, initiative, and self-sacrifice" of the officers and men who salvaged the sunken submarine. Every diver who worked on the *Squalus* received an award—from Congressional Medals of Honor (4), to Navy Crosses (49), to citations from the Secretary of the Navy (4). And, every one of those awards was well earned.

ERIC HANAUER

Eric claims that, thwarted in his childhood ambition to play baseball for the Chicago Cubs by total lack of talent, he focused his attention instead on swimming and scuba diving. A scuba instructor since 1961, Hanauer is an associate professor of physical education at California State University, Fullerton. More than 200 of his articles and photographs have appeared in diving publications worldwide. His book, *The Egyptian Red Sea, A Diver's Guide* (Watersports Publishing, Inc., 1988), is the most comprehensive dive guide on that region ever published. As a swimming coach on the high school and college level, Hanauer developed the grab start, a technique now used by swimmers all over the world.

ERIC HANAUER

Things I Wish
They'd Told Me Before
I Bought My Boat

f I hadn't listened to Mike Curtis that day I probably would be richer in dollars but poorer in experience. Mike, my old diving buddy, had figured we could finally afford to buy a dive boat—not an inflatable, but an honest-to-goodness diving boat with room for tanks and camera gear and everything. A boat that would keep us dry and comfortable the entire 30 miles across the channel to Catalina without being beaten to death.

It sounded too good to be true, but I was hooked. After six weeks of searching—and after selling our souls to the bank—we bought the answer to our dreams. She is a 24-foot Wellcraft Airslot powered by a 350 Chevy engine. She has a cuddy cabin, lots of deck space, and room to store 13 tanks below. Just to make sure everyone knew what she was all about, we christened her the *Deep Freak*.

Seven years later, she has turned out to be everything we expected, our magic carpet to diving adventures. But few people ever realize what they are getting into before they buy a boat. And having a partner can sometimes add the hassles of a marriage with none of the benefits.

Like most boat owners, we had to discover certain things first hand. Prospective boat buyers might profit from our mistakes, so here are a few lessons we learned the hard way.

A Salesman Will Tell You Anything to Sell You a Boat

Salesmen have a sixth sense. They know what you want to hear and will tell you exactly that. With memories of one gasoline crisis fresh in our minds and threats of another one around the corner, we inquired about gas mileage. "Oh, she'll get about five miles per gallon," he replied reassuringly.

That was almost true. The van gets five miles per gallon when towing the *Deep Freak* on the freeway. In the water, the boat gets a bit less—about one and a half with a following swell!

The first time we pulled up to a gas station and watched the tank swallow 120 gallons at 60 cents per, we wondered what we were getting into. A couple of months later, when the Ayotollah shut off the spigot, we knew too well.

Ignorance Is Bliss

You can feel really secure on a boat if you don't know what can happen. Stephen King never wrote a novel as terrifying as Chapman's *Piloting and Seamanship*, the bible for skippers. It was there I first read about pitchpoling. That's what happens when the bow buries itself in a swell. The boat performs a forward somersault, ending up in the pike position. I had nightmares about it for weeks.

We were returning from Catalina Island one afternoon in heavy seas and wind chop. Standing on the deck, I was looking up at the swells about two feet over my six foot head. Bill, the owner of the boat store, was on board. We had taught him to dive in return for some parts and mechanical favors. As the sea got messier and we held the grab rails more tightly, we lost our delusions of immortality and looked to the old mariner for reassurance. "This boat has enough flotation to keep us up for a while if we swamp, doesn't it?"

"Sure," he replied laconically. "For about a minute and a half."

"A Boat Is a Hole in the Water You Pour Money Into."
Another old proverb

When we bought the *Deep Freak*, Mike and I sat down and figured out a monthly budget. First there were payments, insurance, and storage; then there was gas. Add a few miscellaneous bucks for a total of around $300 a month. Split two ways, that didn't sound too bad. The calculations were pretty accurate, as long as she stayed on the trailer.

Once she went into the water, the budget went out the porthole. Everyone knows motors and salt water don't mix. The same can be said for electronics, outdrives, and hulls. Furthermore, boat parts are in the same price range as Porsche parts. And repairs always seem to cost more than the highest estimate. Sometimes you can even outsmart yourself.

At first we worried we might someday launch without the drain plug in place. The solution was to leave the plug in while the boat was stored on its trailer. That worked fine until the first heavy rainstorm. The result was a foot of water in the engine compartment and a drowned starter.

A short time later *Deep Freak* was being kept at a friend's slip.

First time boat owners soon discover it takes a seemingly inexhaustible amount of money to keep these watertoys afloat. Photo by Eric Hanauer.

To save the batteries, they were turned off. Unfortunately, that also turned off the automatic bilge pump. I arrived at the slip one Tuesday for a rare midweek dive. Upon opening the engine compartment to check the oil, I was confronted by two feet of water, submerging the oil pan and the new starter. We had just had a fitting installed for a transom-mounted transducer which hadn't been sealed properly. Had we waited until our normal weekend dive, *Deep Freak* would have been a submarine.

Never Loan Your Boat to a Friend

You probably have a friend like Stan. Although he means well, everything he touches seems to turn into a disaster. Everywhere he goes, the dark cloud of misfortune hangs over his head. When Stan organizes a snipe hunt, he is the one who falls into the cactus. When trying to start a fire, he winds up burning down the campsite.

Being aware of Stan's track record, we should have known better than to loan *Deep Freak* to him. But he is a licensed skipper, so what could possibly go wrong? Just ask Mr. Murphy.

As Stan explained later, there was a funny noise coming from the outdrive. He thought that running for a while at a higher RPM would make it stop. He was right. The noise stopped and so did the outdrive. He returned home ignominiously at the end of a tow rope.

"Check the anchorline, stupid."—Chapman.

We were diving Blue Caverns on the frontside of Catalina Island. The water along the wall was crystal clear, and we were in too much of a hurry to think about checking the anchorline.

Upon surfacing, we realized what a mistake we'd made. *Deep Freak* was 200 yards away, drifting in the general direction of the mainland. My buddies had surfaced about 20 yards behind me, so I was elected to chase her down. With ugly visions of a 26-mile swim home, I sprinted with all the force my fins could generate. Slowly, almost imperceptibly, I gained on her.

Gasping for breath, I finally grabbed the swim step and climbed aboard. Suddenly Phil emerged from the cuddy cabin, rubbing the sleep from his eyes. He wasn't feeling well and, deciding to pass on the dive, had gone to sleep below. I wasn't aware he was on board, but it would have probably taken a crash to awaken him.

"Anything That Can Go Wrong Will Go Wrong."—Murphy

What do hardcore divers do on New Year's Day? Why, they dive, no matter how lively the party the night before. We had made our traditional January 1 dive, and were returning from Catalina. It had been a late start, but the sea was flat and the day was warm and sunny. The marine radio warned about possible Santa Anas—offshore winds that can make coming home a nasty uphill trip. But at 4:00PM the sea was still glassy.

About a third of the way home, a ripple began. By the time we hit halfway, it accelerated to a nasty, wind-driven chop. We had to throttle back to keep from becoming airborne. A strong gust picked up the front seat cushion and blew it overboard. For a moment I thought about going back for it, but realized the consequences of turning around in these seas. By now *Deep Freak* wasn't going over the waves, she was crashing through them. Then the engine began to cough a bit. The cough soon developed into a fullfledged case of bronchitis. It finally sputtered a few times, and quit.

We called the Coast Guard but they had no desire to go out in this mess unless lives were being threatened. After a few false starts, the engine was coaxed back to life, but it wasn't healthy. Four more times the engine quit, and four more times we got it started. By now it was dark, we were soaked and still getting battered, like clothes inside a washing machine. Finally the lights of Newport Harbor came into view. A Coast Guard cutter was waiting inside for us.

We limped back to port and put the *Deep Freak* on her trailer. But, before pulling the plug, I had to look inside the engine compartment. The motor was almost completely submerged. Five times the starter had turned the engine over, even though it was flooded with salt water.

Mike Curtis spent many hours trying to solve the Deep Freak's *mechanical difficulties. Photo by Eric Hanauer.*

The cause of the flood had been a dead bilge pump. There was a manual one on board, but opening the engine box would have let in more water than we could pump out. This had been the first trip after a complete engine overhaul. Needless to say, there is no warranty against stupidity. We should have had a second pump.

Boats Don't Belong on Freeways

I was driving home from work one day, listening to a disc jockey on the car radio. "You won't believe this one, folks. There's a sigalert on the San Diego freeway for a boat in the number three lane." I thought that was pretty funny, especially as he joked about the dummy who didn't know boats belong in the water.

When I arrived home, there was a phone call from Mike. "Guess what happened to your boat," he said. (When there's trouble, it's always my boat.) Mike explained he was bringing *Deep Freak* home after a triumphant opening night of the lobster season. (One dive, six divers, 36 bugs.) Suddenly he heard a screech of brakes and the world started spinning as the trailer jackknifed and his van did a neat 360. The boat skidded off the trailer and laid a 100-yard strip of fiberglass on the freeway. A lady had cut in behind the van, failing to notice there was something big following it. She sideswiped the trailer, causing Mike to lose control. The miraculous thing was that the cars behind managed to avoid the accident and no one was hurt. Traffic was tied up for miles.

It was over an hour before the tow truck arrived and removed the mess. They wrapped chains around the outdrive and the bow cleat to lift *Deep Freak* onto the flatbed. "It's better if you don't watch this," the policeman advised Mike. "If it's any consolation, the insurance company considers towing a part of the accident." In the following day's *Los Angeles Times* was a picture of *Deep Freak* on the freeway, with one of the California Highway Patrol's finest directing traffic around her.

It's times like this when you find out how good your insurance is. Forget the commercials about the concerned agent coming out in wind, sleet, snow, or hail to bring you the check that will rebuild your homestead. All he wants are your premiums. After a couple of weeks of phone calls running the gamut from pleas to threats, the checks finally start coming. It's amazing how much abuse a fiberglass hull can take, and how a transfusion of dollars can bring a boat back from the dead.

As you can see, life with *Deep Freak* has been anything but dull. It hasn't all been disasters, there have been a few triumphs as well. One was finding a virgin wreck and salvaging seven portholes on a single dive. Another was discovering the "Lobster Market," a spot where the big ones hang around just waiting to be grabbed. Others included diving some of the garden spots of Southern California: Farnsworth Bank, Ship Rock, Santa Barbara Island, and hidden wrecks like the *Moody*. Dolphins in the bow wave or watching gray whales on their way to Baja are wonderful as are late morning starts and sunny days on and under the water with a few good friends.

In the old days, as we idled through Newport Harbor in a tiny inflatable, we would look up at the big yachts and powerboats and say disdainfully, "We're having a lot more fun than they are." Today on *Deep Freak*, we say it with more conviction.

For some, there is no thrill to compare with visiting a virgin shipwreck—one that few or none have seen before. Rod Farb is such a person. Thus, you can imagine the excitement he felt when he visited the Civil War ironclad *Monitor* on his birthday in June 1990. She lies 230 feet under the sea—way beyond the limits of most sport divers—and the expedition Farb organized to visit her took a great deal of planning.

Rod is a diver of considerable experience, having taken up the sport in his teens. He is also an expert on wrecks. His first book, *Shipwrecks: Diving the Graveyard of the Atlantic*, was published in 1984. A second book, *Guide to Shipwrecks: North Carolina*, came off the presses in 1990.

ROD FARB

Descent to the Monitor

W hen the beginning of the Civil War was signaled by the bombardment and capture of Fort Sumter, South Carolina, President Lincoln ordered a U.S. naval blockade. It was to cover the entire coastline of the south from Virginia to Texas. Even before the outbreak of hostilities, the largely non-industrialized South was heavily dependent upon ocean shipping to bring it the necessities of life. Lincoln reasoned that if southern ports were closed, then vital military supplies would be unavailable to the Confederacy, thus severely hindering its war effort.

After the fall of Fort Sumter in April 1861, the Confederates captured the Gosport Navy Yard at Norfolk, Virginia. The largest and most modern shipyard of its day, Gosport was taken after Union troops burned and abandoned the facility, including the frigate USS *Merrimac*. The *Merrimac* had been in drydock awaiting repair of its condemned boilers and engines. Following capture by the Confederates, the *Merrimac's* superstructure was taken down to its main deck and the ship was converted into an ironclad. It was cheaper and less time consuming to convert an already existing ship than to build one, especially since the South lacked the ironworks for the job. Once word of the *Merrimac's* conversion became known in Washington, DC, Lincoln immediately asked for plans to build a Union ironclad.

Ironclads were not new at the time of the Civil War. Britain and France had built a few ironclad vessels as early as 1853. In 1854, John Ericsson, a Swedish engineer and designer, had submitted plans for such a ship to Napoleon III for his battles in the Crimean War. The plans were never accepted and sat in limbo for many years until the American Civil war.

After much urging, Ericsson answered the call from Lincoln. His design for the U.S. ironclad was quite similar to the one he had done for the French. The deck was to be awash and there was a revolving gun turret. After much debate and with reluctance, Ericsson's design was accepted by the Navy and work was begun on the ship in New York. The design called for several unique features that had never been seen before on a naval warship. These included a revolving gun turret that was 20 feet in diameter with 8 inch thick iron walls and armed with two 11-inch Dahlgren guns, a unique anchor, underwater anchor windlass room, protected anchor well, pressurized engine room, forced air draft boiler, a special valve for operating a marine head (toilet) located below the waterline, no exposed deck, and a pilothouse forward with a sight-slit for viewing.

The 173 foot long, 981 ton warship was finally launched on January 30, 1862. Some of those present on that day did not believe the all-iron ship would float, but when she slid into the water, she drew ten feet and floated within three inches of where Ericsson had predicted she would.

Commissioned on February 25, 1862, under the command of Lt. J. John Worden, the ironclad, named *Monitor* by its inventor, had been built in 147 days from contract to commissioning. But, according to the terms of the contract, the *Monitor* had to prove herself in battle before she could be accepted by the Navy. With only nine days of sea trials between commissioning and sailing for Hampton Roads, Virginia, there was little time to

An early rendering of the Monitor. *Designed by John Ericsson, a Swedish designer/engineer, it was launched on January 30, 1862.*

train her all-volunteer crew members. They men had many problems learning to operate the newfangled machinery on board the strange and unfamiliar craft. Nonetheless, the *Monitor* departed New York under tow on March 6, 1862, and headed for Hampton Roads. She arrived there on the evening of March 8 after nearly sinking twice on the harrowing sea journey.

Meanwhile, the *Merrimac*, renamed CSS *Virginia*, was undergoing hurried completion at Norfolk. Loaded with workers until sailing time, the 310 foot long ironclad steamed out of the shipyard to meet the blockading Union Navy at Hampton Roads at noon on March 8. Prior to departure, none of her guns had been fired and her engines hardly tested at all. Because of her length it took thirty minutes to turn the cumbersome ship at a top speed of five knots. The Federals feared that once clear of the Union Navy at Hampton Roads, the CSS *Virginia* would steam up the East Coast, bombarding northern ports, and then up the Potomac to Washington, DC, to bombard the nation's capitol. Caught completely unaware by the *Virginia* as she steamed out of the Elizabeth River to meet the Union blockading fleet, the Union frigates USS *Cumberland* and USS *Congress* were sunk in short order by the ironclad. By now the Union fleet was in complete disarray and the *Virginia* took full advantage of the confusion. Making for the frigate USS *Minnesota* as dusk fell, the Confederate ironclad decided to withdraw to await dawn. As dusk came and the *Virginia* steamed back up the Elizabeth River, the USS *Monitor* steamed into Hampton Roads, prepared to meet the Confederate threat.

Suffering its worst defeat, the Union fleet initially did not recognize the *Monitor*. However, soon signals announced that the Union ironclad had arrived. The fleet waited uneasily throughout the night. More than one Union sailor wondered if this ship that looked like a water tank on a flat deck could possibly be successful in battle against the formidable *Virginia*. The following morning, her decks stripped of all gear except the gun turret and the pilothouse, the *Monitor* prepared for battle.

At half-past seven on the morning of March 9, the *Virginia* got underway and headed for the *Minnesota*. Positioning herself between the *Virginia* and the *Minnesota*, the *Monitor* steamed toward the Confederate ironclad. The *Virginia* started firing almost immediately but the *Monitor* held her fire until she was directly alongside the Confederate ship.

For nearly five hours the two ironclads shot at each other, often at point blank range. Although outgunned ten guns to two, the *Monitor* could easily outmaneuver the longer and more unwieldy *Virginia*. Since the *Monitor's* gun turret could revolve, the ship did not have to change course to change the aim of her two cannons. The *Virginia*, on the other hand, had to steer her 310 foot length where she wanted her ten guns to fire.

After five hours of battle, during which neither side inflicted mortal wounds upon the other, a shot from the *Virginia* struck the *Monitor's* pilothouse at the side-slit, blinding Lt. Worden—the

The battle of the Union ironclad Monitor *(left) and the Confederate ironclad* Merrimac *took place on March 9, 1862. The battle was a draw.*

commanding officer. In the 20 or so minutes it took to get Lt. Greene, the executive officer of the *Monitor*, from the turret to the pilothouse to take charge of the ship, she drifted aimlessly.

The *Virginia*, leaking badly and perceiving that her adversary had withdrawn from the battle, turned and headed for the Elizabeth River and Norfolk.

Once under control, the *Monitor* fired a couple of shots at the departing *Virginia* and proceeded to come alongside the *Minnesota*.

Thus ended the first naval battle between ironclads. From a tactical point of view the *Monitor* won the battle because it kept the *Virginia* from sinking the *Minnesota*. From a strategic point of view, the battle was a draw. However, the battle's influence on naval warfare and warship design was monumental. The French and British ships observing the battle were left with the knowledge that the day of wooden warships powered by sail and mast were over. The future of modern warships lay in iron armor and steam/propeller propulsion.

Southern newspapers touted the battle as a victory for the South, while northern papers gave the victory to the *Monitor*. Many believe that the *Monitor* singlehandedly saved the Union from defeat by preventing the *Virginia* from leaving Hampton Roads. If the *Virginia* had successfully routed Union forces on the Eastern Seaboard, European nations, who had been holding back their support for the South because they did not believe she could win the war, may have come to her aid.

The *Monitor* and the *Virginia* were never to meet again to settle the question of which was the best. Later in 1862, the *Virginia* was burned by Confederates when Norfolk was captured by the Union. The *Monitor* returned to the Navy Yard in Washington and was repaired and refurbished for future battles. In November of 1862, the *Monitor* returned to Hampton Roads to await further orders. Other *Monitor*-type ships were completed by the Union after the famous battle and, eventually, the U.S. Navy would commission 33 ironclads of Ericsson's design.

On December 24, 1862, the *Monitor* was ordered to Beaufort, North Carolina, under tow of the USS *Rhode Island*. Departing Hampton Roads on December 29, the two ships had an uneventful trip south for the first day and a half. South of Cape Henry, early on December 30, the seas worsened. By the afternoon the ships were nearing Cape Hatteras in the midst of a fierce storm. The *Monitor* began taking on large amounts of water. Her pumps were barely able to keep up with the incoming water. Having her towing lines cut and her anchor dropped doomed the iron ship to a fate the CSS *Virginia* had not been able to accomplish. As the water in the ship rose and reached the boilers, the *Monitor's* pumps became ineffective. It was clear the ironclad would sink. At about 9:00PM, the *Monitor* crew members used a red lantern to signal the USS *Rhode Island* to come to their assistance. At great risk to their own lives, crewmen in boats from the *Rhode Island* were able to save 47 of the 63 officers and men on board the ironclad. At 1:30AM on December 31, the *Monitor* sank approximately 20 miles SE of Cape Hatteras. The ship that singlehandedly saved the Union had perished.

For more than a century, the location of the *Monitor* remained a mystery. In August of 1973, Duke University's research vessel, *Eastward*, sponsored by the National Geographic Society, began a search for the ironclad. Using the navigational track of the *Rhode Island* as the basis for its search, the expedition discovered a wreck in 230 feet of water. It was to remain unclear whether this wreck was the *Monitor* until April of 1974. At that time another expedition funded by the National Geographic Society aboard the *Alcoa Sea Probe*, a high-tech deep-ocean research vessel, returned to the site and positively identified the wreck as that of the *Monitor*.

In 1975, the site was nominated and placed on the National Register of Historic Places and, on the 113th anniversary of the ship's launching, the *Monitor* site was established as the nation's first Marine Sanctuary. It is managed by the Department of Commerce through its National Oceanic and Atmospheric Administration (NOAA).

There have been several research expeditions to the *Monitor* since its discovery. In 1977, the red lantern was recovered. In 1979, the Cousteaus tried to film the site but divers failed to reach the wreck because of extremely poor conditions. Later that year, Harbor Branch Oceanographic Institution's RV *Johnson* conducted the most extensive work by divers on the site. In 1983 the *Monitor's* anchor was retrieved and is now on display at the Mariners Museum in Newport News, Virginia. Extensive

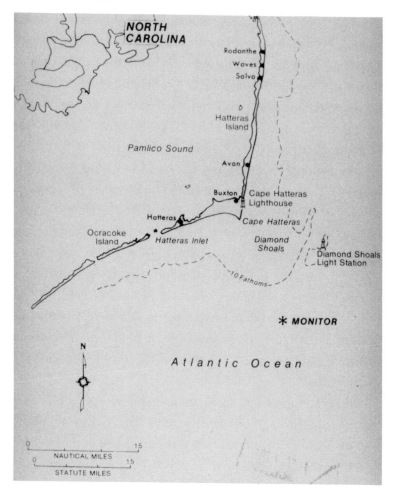

Map showing the location of the Monitor. *Illustration by Rod Farb.*

videography and photography of the site had been done over the years but the results have been less than desirable because of unpredictable conditions and inflexible schedules of the various expeditions doing work there.

In 1986, I submitted a proposal to NOAA to visit the *Monitor* to photograph and videograph the site. The proposal was accepted but the plan of using air for the dives ran counter to the

NOAA Diving Office's regulations. These regulations do not permit diving deeper than 130 feet using air. At NOAA's suggestion, I resubmitted the plan, substituting mixed gas (a mixture of helium and oxygen), which was acceptable to NOAA.

Meanwhile, in December 1989, an Administrative Law Judge ruled that NOAA could not use its Diving Office regulations to forbid diving on the *Monitor*. This opened the door to diving the *Monitor* using air. Not only are the logistics of using air simpler than mixed gas, air is much cheaper. Finally, in February 1990, I was awarded one of the first permits issued to a civilian to dive the *Monitor* site.

The Expedition

The Expedition received equipment support from many corporate sponsors. U.S. Divers supplied all of the diving equipment. Other sponsors included IBM, Xerox Imaging, Hasselblad, Amphibico, Sony, Underwater Kinetics, Zodiac, Evinrude, Light and Motion, Orca Industries, Southern Nikonos, Probe Electronics, Equinox, Bio-Scan, Poseidon, and Helix.

Being the first civilian to dive the *Monitor* was a fluke. It was ironic. My expedition was scheduled by NOAA to be the second dive to the wreck but as luck would have it, we ended up being the first.

My permit ran from June 1 to August 31 and I scheduled four ten day cruises to the *Monitor* during that period. I gave NOAA the first two days of my permit time so it could dive the site in a four person submarine, the *Johnson Sea-Link*. The submersible was launched from the RV *Johnson* on contract from Harbor Branch Oceanographic Institution.

The two days turned out to be perfect for this operation. The calm, clear waters yielded some of the best video of the wreck that NOAA had been able to achieve since it began managing the site in 1975. It was good luck for NOAA but bad luck for me, as I could have been diving there instead.

My first dive was scheduled for June 5 but a strong northeast wind prevented us from leaving the dock that day. However, we knew from our experience diving other deep wrecks in the area that the day following cessation of a northeast wind would be optimal time to dive the *Monitor*. The water would be current free and clear. Late on the evening of June 5, the winds stopped. Weather-wise, we were definitely on for the 6th. I was especially happy because that was also my 44th birthday.

Anticipation was at a fever pitch the next morning as we loaded the DV *Sea Fox*, a 55 foot vessel, moored at Teach's Lair Marina in Hatteras, North Carolina. The skipper was Captain Doogie Pledger, one of the best on the Carolina coast. John McKenney and the Jack McKenney Productions crew were on board to make a documentary film for television about the *Monitor* and this expedition. All of their equipment had to be loaded on board, including a large generator to power 3,000 watts of lights via 600 feet of heavy cable. Twenty-four sets of twin 80 scuba tanks with a single 30 as a pony bottle, tanks containing 500 cubic feet of oxygen for the final stage of decompression, 4 complete sets of decompression hoses, a large decompression platform, buoys, anchors, 600 feet of anchor line for the buoys, dive gear, ice chests, a 16 foot Zodiac inflatable, a 25-horse-power Evinrude outboard motor, 10 divers, 6 support personnel, the captain, two mates and Lt. Ilene Byron, the NOAA observer, were placed aboard the nearly overloaded dive boat.

By 6:30AM we were underway. The site was 19 miles out. The water was flat and calm with not a ripple in site. There was bright sunshine and the day was cloudless. It was my birthday and a perfect day so far.

Two hours later we were three miles from the site. The surface water temperature was 71°F. Within the next mile, the water became azure blue as its temperature rose to 80°F. It was loaded with sargassum weed, a sure sign of clear, Gulf Stream water. One mile from the site, we stopped to call the Coast Guard at Hatteras to tell them we were entering the sanctuary and about to begin diving operations. A short while later we arrived at the site. The Loran numbers NOAA had provided were not correct. It took Captain Doogie about 20 minutes to locate the wreck. There was absolutely no current on the site. Unbelievable! my 44th birthday, the *Monitor* wreck site, flat calm seas, crystal clear, 80°F water and no current. We could scarcely believe our luck.

For months we had worked out the details of the first dive. It was complicated by the fact that NOAA will not permit a boat to anchor within 500 feet of the wreck. We devised and had a plan approved whereby the captain of the *Sea Fox* would keep the vessel directly over the wreck while the support crew lowered a single 200 pound anchor, specially built for the purpose, to 20 feet above the wreck. Cameraman, John McKenney, soundman, Pete Manchee, and I were to descend the line to the anchor. If it was clear below, we would signal the boat, via the Equinox Dolphin system, to lower the anchor to the bottom and give us slack in the line. Then, by means of a 250 pound liftbag and a tank of air provided for the purpose, we could move and place the anchor at the approved 75 foot distance from the turret on the northeast side of the wreck.

The current on the *Monitor* site flows basically southwest to northeast. Positioning the anchor on the northeast end of the wreck would place it down-current and out of harm's way.

Now that we were at the site under perfect conditions, we began to put our plan into effect. Before starting the anchoring operation, we had to launch the Zodiac. This done, we loaded it with the Evinrude outboard motor, a large 330 cubic foot oxygen cylinder, the generator, 600 feet of cable, the cable lights, decompression platform, decompression hoses, and a cylinder with 100 cubic feet of air, which was to be hung at 60 feet for out of air emergencies. Once loaded and all of the lines, air cylinder, and decompression platform in position, the Zodiac slowly motored a few feet away from the *Sea Fox* to await the lowering of the first anchor.

The anchorline was attached to the first 200 pound anchor and marked at the 210 foot length. The crew quickly lowered the anchor, a liftbag, and scuba cylinder to the appropriate depth. McKenney, Manchee, and I rapidly descended through crystal clear water to the anchor. I had a Sony housing with the Hi-Band video camera, McKenney had a 16mm film camera, and Manchee had the Equinox signaling device.

I was in the lead and at 180 feet I began to see the wreck. The site was undulating, dancing around. I blinked and kept descending. I knew how I deal with narcosis. I do deep dives regularly and although narcosis is there I always function just fine. I had never seen undulating wrecks before. What was going on? As I passed 200 feet, I saw what was happening. The wreck, sitting in 75 to 100 feet of visibility, was completely shrouded by a thick layer of baitfish. The shimmering mass of fishes took the shape of the wreck site and was definitely undulating. I was relieved and had to stifle a laugh.

At 210 feet I had an unobstructed view of the wreck and of our anchor. Captain Doogie had placed the *Sea Fox* 40 feet off the port side of the wreck and the anchor hung in perfect position. Nothing was below it. While watching for McKenney and Manchee, I dropped down to the wreck and began videotaping the site. I was stunned. At a depth of 235 feet, it was beautiful; like a tropical oasis in an ocean bottom desert. It was a living reef. My video light illuminated the most beautiful, colorful scene I had ever witnessed. Narcosis made it even more vivid. Shades of yellow, red, pink, brown, green, and blue colored the wreckage. McKenney had arrived by then and began filming me videotaping the wreck. With clenched fists raised over our heads, we signaled victory. We were the first on the site since Cousteau. It was without a doubt the finest birthday present I had ever received in my life.

McKenney signaled me back to the anchor. After all, we had made this dive to film the lowering and placement of the anchor. What seemed like the passing of hours had actually been only a matter of minutes. We looked up and there was Manchee patiently waiting for us to get back to him and signal the boat. After what seemed like an eternity, the anchor was lowered to the sand and Pete effortlessly moved it into position without the liftbag.

On the surface we knew that by now the crew had handed the anchorline to the Zodiac where other crew members secured it to the large buoy that one of the divers, John Renfro, had built for the purpose. McKenney filmed Manchee swimming around the turret and more of the wreck. By now our time was up. We descended to the surface and prepared for an hour or so of decompression. We were ecstatic! Our plan had worked perfectly.

After we got back to the *Sea Fox*, the second dive team, John Renfro, Charles Capps, and Karen Rogers, prepared the second 200 pound anchor and sent it down to join the first. Then they ascended, secured both anchors together and did a quick survey of the wreck. With the anchoring chore complete, the first day's operation was a tremendous success. By virtue of her dive to the site, Rogers became the first woman in history to dive the *Monitor*. The entire team was very happy for her and her accomplishment. She had trained for this dive for months and had become one of our strongest divers.

Over the next few days we would make six more dives to the wreck. Sometimes we made two dives a day to 235 feet with a three and a half hour surface interval. The Monitor 2 dive computer, which we all used, worked flawlessly.

Oxygen decompression at 20 feet was essential for this kind of diving. Chris Wachholz of the Diver Alert Network made repetitive dives to the site and was pleased with the decompression profiles. Wachholz is convinced that in-water oxygen decompression is essential to safe decompression diving.

For the most part, all of the dives went well. But, we did have problems. On one dive, one of the film crew, who was handling McKenney's light cable, became entangled at 200 feet and ran out of air before he could be freed. In a moment of panic, he made a rapid ascent using his buddy's air and went directly to the surface without any decompression. Luckily, his bottom time had been short. He came through the episode without any problems, although he clearly had a bad scare. We changed the way the film crew handled the cable after that. Then, fishermen stole our buoy and we had to dive for the anchorline and fit it to another buoy. But, we managed to overcome all of the obstacles and make the dives.

During June, I led two cruises to the *Monitor* and the dives went very well. All of the divers were pleased to be a part of the first of two groups to visit the famous shipwreck.

The Monitor *lies upside down, the turret is visible at the bottom center of the photo. Photo by Rod Farb.*

The Wreck

The USS *Monitor* lies about ten miles inshore of the western edge of the Gulf Stream. By virtue of her proximity to its tropical Caribbean waters, she is a living reef. Colorful corals and sponges grow in abundance on her collapsed structure.

When the ironclad sank, she turned upside down. The impact sheared the turret from the deck and it went sliding to the port side of the stern. Initially, the lower hull, which was elevated, probably rose 15 feet or so above the sand. Immersed in corrosive salt water for more than 128 years, degraded by marine organisms, battered by hurricanes and ocean storms, raked by

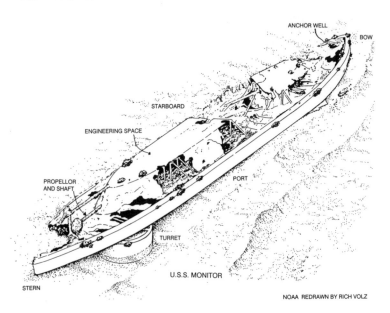

A drawing of the Monitor *site. Illustration by Rich Volz, Farb Montior Expedition.*

incessant strong currents and, most likely, blown up by depth charges during World War II, the venerable ironclad has all but collapsed to the bottom in a pile of hull plates, iron ribs, machinery, and the like. The tilt to the starboard has buried the armor belt on that side but the turret still provides support for the armor belt of the port side.

From above the site, the remains possess irregular features of a ship larger than one would have imagined the ironclad to have been. It was no wonder so many people doubted its ability to float when the ironclad was first launched.

The *Monitor's* stern is mostly gone, but the remains of the propeller shaft and the framing for the rudder may still be seen. The propeller and its shaft have been displaced from their original position but are still present. The bottom of the hull is intact aft of the single amidships bulkhead that supported the turret. This part of the hull is supported by the engine, two boilers, pumps, machinery and equipment in the engine room and boiler area, the so-called engineering space. In this space, the engine, boilers, pumps, and other machinery are still intact. The sides of the hull in this area have deteriorated and only hull frame members survive. Several of the hull plates along each side of the engineering space and a few on its upper surface are missing, exposing several hull ribs. The standing portion runs forward only a short distance of 40 feet or less. Today, the engineering space is succumbing to the effect of years under the sea. Corrosion and the force of gravity are tilting the hull downhill to the starboard. Its ribs are buckling as well, indicating that the structure is settling. The tilt has caused a few of the hull plates on the upper surface to shear their retaining rivets and to be displaced.

Forward of the main bulkhead, the hull has collapsed extensively into the interior of the ship. There are a number of artifacts visible near the pilothouse, thought to be equipment and fittings once stored in the crew's quarters and wardroom.

The port side armor belt is intact and visible from the stern to the bow. There is significant separation between the armor belt and the hull to which it was attached. At the sand it is possible to swim all the way around the turret under what was the deck of the ship. There are what appear to be two hatches visible on the deck in this area, but these may be the ventilator openings or the smokestack exhausts.

Much of the port side hull remains standing from the turret forward to the bow. The portion of the vessel that is bounded between the port and starboard sides and forward of the engineering space lies in rubble. In this area, hull plates, hull ribs,

The engineering space on the Monitor *as it looks today. Photo by Rod Farb.*

pipes, broken machinery, and the like are piled upon another in a helter-skelter fashion common to all broken-up iron ships.

At the bow, the anchor well is visible but has lost much of its symmetry. Rounding the bow and proceeding to the stern along the starboard side, there is a manifest difference in the condition of the wreck from that of the port side. No armor belt is visible and there is a remarkable loss of structure all the way to the stern. The ribs of the lower hull, containing the engineering space, run into the sand on this side and several of the hull plates are missing. At the stern, sand has filled the wreck from starboard to port.

Throughout the site, wreckage is covered with calcareous material several inches thick and with corals and sponges. Large amberjacks patrol the wreckage and curious black seabass move in and out of the nooks and crannies with ease. Butterflyfish and blue angelfish appear unexpectedly and small baitfish, mackerel scad, often obscure a view of the site.

HILLARY HAUSER

Just out of college in 1966, Hillary was visiting her mother in Santa Barbara when she met Glenn Miller, the owner/captain of a charter dive boat. He introduced her to diving, changing her life and enriching ours. Hillary has written six books and innumerable magazine articles. Her credits include *Skin Diver*, *National Geographic*, *Westways*, *Ocean Realm*, *Islands*, and the Santa Barbara *News-Press*, where she was reporter for several years. Her latest book, *The Adventurous Aquanaut*, was published in the spring of 1990.

Hillary's writing is frequently laced with humor, as is most any conversation with her. She has a remarkable sense of adventure and a curiosity about all things. These have led her from California's Sierra Nevada mountains to the sinkholes of Australia—and numerous places in between! She lives in Santa Barbara.

HILLARY HAUSER

Gold in Them Thar Hills

T he trail to Canyon Creek snakes its way for a mile down the side of a steep, heavily wooded canyon in the Sierra Nevadas, California's mother lode country. It is so steep you can touch ground with your uphill hand without bending over and if you lose the trail you are liable to fly down the entire mountain by the seat of your pants. I know this is true because I flew down half the mountain toward Canyon Creek by the seat of my own pants until I was stopped by a tree. The thick layer of dried pine needles and leaves made the slope as slippery as ice, and since no one had been on the trail for what looked like months, traction was nonexistent. My knees shook uncontrollably as I looked down the rest of the hill into the dark of the canyon. There was only one way to stay on the path and that was by watching closely for the old blaze marks that had been chopped years before into the thick bark of ancient pine trees by hopeful seekers of gold.

The man I had just married was a reincarnated '49er, a seasoned adventurer who had an uncanny knack for finding gold. That June morning in 1968, Dick Anderson's internal calendar sped back to the year 1849, when thousands of fortune-seeking adventurers descended on the California mother lode to search for gold.

Dick Anderson

This Canyon Creek trip introduced me to the slippery world of treasure, where men scratch, blast, dig, dynamite, pump, and drill their way through river banks and seabeds in search of the great something-for-nothing. Dick had access to a mining claim in Canyon Creek, which is near the North Fork of California's Yuba River, east of Sacramento on Highway 49 outside Downieville. He hadn't been to Canyon Creek in years. It was here that he and his friend Donald Carter spent every summer years before. The two of them fared pretty well at Canyon Creek. Dick even came away with a sizable amount of nuggets to show for his work. Then Carter fell down a mine shaft in Nevada and died. That cooled Dick's gold fever, but only for a time. Gold-seekers have a history of such disasters and accept them as part of this glittery game of chance. Dick could hardly wait, in fact, to start digging again once he made up his mind to it.

Before starting down the trail to the bottom of the canyon we had checked in with Cliff Laurent, the deputy sheriff at the Cal-Ida sawmill near the top of the trail. This stop was required by law. If we accidentally ignited a forest fire, there would be a clue as to who did it, but more importantly, if we didn't check out after a reasonable length of time, someone would come looking for us. As I slipped and slid down the trail behind Dick, I wondered if Cliff Laurent would really go to all the trouble. I was convinced that no one could *ever* find us. Our Volkswagen bus had been carefully buried in the trees so that the bears wouldn't eat it; and right then I was sure that they'd skip the bus anyway and head out to snack on us. In that place we were so alone I couldn't help but think how easy it would have been to disappear off the face of the earth without anyone knowing it.

Our dog Igor was having a fine time. A poodle-terrier mix, Igor was hardly a dog of the woods and feared everything, but as a trail scout he did fine. He ran ahead and back in a fraction of the time it took us to navigate one way. I would stop to rest while Dick tried to find the overgrown and faded blaze marks. Igor would run off, run back, run in little circles, look out into the deep woods, look worried, and then whine. I identified with him a lot, but I never said a word. New brides always want to be good sports.

On my back I carried a lot of the groceries and some of the diving gear. Dick hauled more of the diving equipment, plus pans, picks, supplies, gasoline, and more groceries. On top of it all, he dragged a mattress behind him, saying that since no one had been to the cabin in five years, any leftover supplies would be gone, used by stray fishermen or prospectors—or eaten by the rats. He was sure that the rats had eaten the mattress that had been left there. These rats were ferocious, he said, and from everything I heard about them I figured they might have eaten the cabin itself. Bus-eating bears and cabin-eating rats: this had to be the mother lode version of *The Call of the Wild* and I was Buck, stolen from my comfortable home and pressed into service as a trail beast.

When I saw the cabin I was greatly cheered. It sat back from the creek, 100 feet or so, up a little trail in the trees. It was the real live log kind that measured about 15 by 20 feet, and it had a creaky wooden door crowned with a set of old reindeer antlers at the top. A single window faced the river. Just outside the door was a tiny dirt terrace and on its uphill side was a wood-burning stovetop set into rocks. There was still a neat stack of old wood underneath a rickety workbench to the right of the stove. The river in front of the cabin formed a deep pool that was cold and crystal clear, and Dick said it was full of trout.

I looked at everything and felt much better. Igor wasn't so sure. He kept backing up and growling and I half expected something wild to leap out of the woods and attack us. Animals are supposed to have uncanny instincts about other animals lurking nearby, so I was always watching Igor's displays of uncanny instincts. The only trouble with this alarm system was the Igor was deathly afraid of things like falling leaves and rolling stones, and by this time he had become a bundle of dog nerves.

The inside of the cabin was a wreck. Even though the supplies had been hung from the rafters years before so that the rats couldn't get at them, the vermin had found plenty of other things to chew on. The entire room was a rat's nest. Everywhere we looked was shredded paper, cloth, bits of this, piles of that, pine needles, wood chips nibbled and chewed. Dust and dirt covered the wood plank floor and the crude shelves that held big glass jars of five-year-old rations were covered with rat trails.

Igor growled and backed up from the door. Had I known what he was trying to tell me I might have growled and backed up, too.

In about four or five hours we had the cabin completely swept and cleaned, our new supplies in, the old ones out, thrown on the rubbish pile at the far end of the outside terrace. The crowning touch was when Dick installed the mattress on top of the old, rusty bedsprings. Igor wasn't taking any chances and immediately rushed up on the bed and didn't move for the rest of the day or evening.

Before dark we lugged in several pails of water from the river for cooking and washing and took a brisk swim in the freezing, clear pool in front of the cabin. Then we set about cooking dinner, which was some magic thing that expanded from a small box onto a mismatched pair of tin plates. This, together with boiled river water, was as wonderful as cordon bleu and champagne—all because we were in the woods.

That night, Dick hung his revolver on the tree-limb bedpost and turned down the kerosene lamp until it went out. Igor was asleep at my feet and I was feeling quite fine. I was blissfully tired and almost dropping off to sleep.

Suddenly the bedsprings began to rattle furiously. I sat straight up and Igor disappeared down the crack between the bed and the wall.

"Dick!" I said. "What's that?"

"Don't know, just a minute."

He fumbled around in the dark. The bedsprings rattled again, more violently this time.

"Iggy, where are you?"

The bedsprings rattled again.

"Rats," said Dick. "I can't find the matches."

Whatever was making the springs rattle like that had to be a gorilla.

"Hold on, I found them."

Dick lit the kerosene lamp and when the light came on I was instantly horrified. Sitting on the cross beams of the wall at the foot of the bed was the biggest rat I'd ever seen. Its eyes glowed in the light of the lamp and it looked at us, transfixed and evil. I was speechless.

Dick, being a reincarnated '49er, knew exactly what to do. He reached for his revolver. The rat was immediately dead. Then Dick holstered the gun and turned off the light.

I was stricken by dumbness undefinable. The dog jumped back up to his place at my feet and I was now supposed to go to sleep. There was no way on earth I could close my eyes. I lost every shred of blessed tiredness I had earned and I lay there in the sleeping bag bed, stiff as a board, the image of that splattered rat indelibly etched into my brain. I was alone for what seemed like hours with the image of that rat.

What I hadn't learned yet was that rat-shooting is nothing when you're looking for gold.

For the next week Dick and I sniffed and sniped, which are two ways of picking around for river gold. A sniffer, which sort of resembles a giant turkey baster, will suck up any flakes or small nuggets that might be stuck in the cracks of a river bed. More often we sniped, using a fireplace poker to scrape out the cracks and crevices.

Gold found in rivers and streams is called placer gold (a word that rhymes with plaster). Essentially it is gold that has been getting stuck for millions of years in the natural riffles of the river bed—the cracks, crevices, and deep potholes. Dick taught me how to spot likely looking cracks for gold—cracks which run from one side of the river to the other, but which are hard to spot because they are often covered with surface soil. We could usually see some part of them if we traced them carefully from either side of the river. Once we located such a crack, we'd put on our masks and snorkels, and dip our heads underwater for a look. The water was only three or four feet deep in the area we were diving, but it was always swift. If I got swept away, Dick advised me to relax and enjoy the ride until I got to the nearest falls. At that point, he said, I should start worrying.

Once underwater we'd snipe the loose dirt and sand from the crevice into the gold pan. The gold pan was the essential tool. All the excavated sand and gravel went into it, and when we had collected enough of it, Dick would begin to pan. Panning is done just like in the movies. Dick dipped the pan into the river, then swirled and dipped again and again, to wash off the top layer of sediment, picking out the larger rocks and dipping again. When he finally reached black sand at the bottom of the pan, I was leaning over him like a hawk. Suddenly I realized I had caught a little of the thing called gold fever. When a few tiny chips and flakes of gold appeared I shrieked as if we'd unearthed Fort Knox.

A few chips and flakes were not enough for Dick, so one morning he dug out the old rusty parts of his dredge from inside the cabin. Dredges are called "suckers" among gold divers, because they are essentially underwater vacuum cleaners that quickly remove all the overburden—the sand and gravel that sit on top of bedrock where the gold is trapped. Our dredge had a lightweight metal vacuum tube at one end and a sluice box with the riffle tray at the other. When the dredge was fired up, water ran through the sluice box and into the riffle tray at the other end. The dirt, sand, and gravel shoveled into the sluice box were sent through the riffles in a wash of mud. Any gold in the sand and gravel would sink and get caught in the coarse metal mesh. With this dredge Dick and I were ready for some big nuggets.

With a sluice box and dredge we didn't bother with turkey basters or fireplace pokers. We used shovels. We first had to find a likely-looking spot where gold might have settled into the bedrock, and the likely-looking spot we picked was within the roots of a big tree near the river bank. Dick set up the dredge and connected the pump, and we both proceeded to dig. And dig. We shoveled so much dirt into that sluice box that I was sure we would reach China by noon. I developed a severe case of blisters and so I volunteered to serve as cheerleader, watching over the riffle tray for signs of color. I have to admit I became a fickle hunter of gold. By the end of the afternoon I had taken up trout fishing instead, using a jar of iridescent orange salmon eggs as bait. It turned out to be a great day for me. I ended up with four trout. Dick ended up with a hole the size of a mass grave, a set of rippling muscles and toughened hands.

By the end of our adventure in the woods, I had become an excellent trout fisherwoman, sniper, and digger of holes; and I hadn't been swept over the falls. Dick and I left Canyon Creek with one small vial of flakes, not enough to pay for the gas we'd fueled the dredge pump with, but one has to be a good sport about such things. One has to be a good sport, also, about climbing a mile out of a steep canyon. Hiking down that trail was rough, but it was child's play in comparison to the hike up. Each step was a deep knee-bend and we performed hours and hours of them.

Igor was the happiest dog I'd ever seen. He repeatedly ran up ahead of us and back with cheery barks. On one hand, I think he was reminding us that there are some advantages to being a

Using a dredge to look for gold in a river is a cold, often unrewarding pastime. The hope of finding a nugget or two, however slim, eggs the prospector on. Photo by Bonnie J. Cardone.

dog—like having four legs—and on the other hand, I think he was letting us know he was glad to get out of the woods and back to the city. Sometimes dogs just have no sense of adventure at all.

Dick and I went to Canyon Creek several times during the next few years. It always seemed just enough gold appeared to make us go back for more, but never enough to make us believe that we went for the gold alone. I finally realized that the value of gold was not the sole reason for seeking it, but that the act of looking for it propelled me. If a man is lucky enough to strike gold, it is a near mystical indication that he is favored by the Hand of Fate. The dice are not always rolled for fortune alone, but because man likes to test himself on many different levels.

When I first started going to Canyon Creek I was a young bride out for a spree in the woods, accompanying a husband who had a nose for gold. I didn't know then that in all that digging the seeds of adventure were being planted within me, seeds that would bloom later when I was no longer with him and during times of choice between the safe and the uncertain. In these later years, I opted more and more for the uncertain, because I sensed that, like gold, the richest experiences of life were often in a hidden lode just beneath the surface of the obvious.

Devil's Hole

I looked at the sign, "Beware of Wild Dogs and Buckshot!" and then I looked at my friend Jack. How we were going to proceed from this point was entirely up to him. Out in a remote corner of the Amargosa Desert of Nevada, one didn't just drive into a place that had a sign like that without giving it a little thought. On the other hand, we were lost, had almost torn the car apart on wretched roads, and even though it was almost dark, it was a sweltering 100°F in the shade. This was the first hint of civilization we had seen in a while.

We were looking for Devil's Hole, an enormous, water-filled earthquake fault that is part of the Death Valley National Monument. We figured something like Devil's Hole would be easy to pick out in the parched, flat landscape, but we figured wrong. After zig-zagging the desert for a good part of the afternoon, our good dispositions were evaporating with the outside heat.

At the very bottom of our increasing uneasiness was the fact that once we found Devil's Hole we weren't sure what we would be able to do with it. We had tried for weeks to get permission to dive and photograph it, but National Park Service restrictions were severe. A number of divers had died in the hole, and it was also the only home in the world for the endangered Devil's Hole pupfish. Just as the snail darter had halted the mega-million dollar construction of a dam in Tennessee, the Devil's Hole pupfish has stopped the pumping of water from underneath the Amargosa Desert.

It was all a heated matter and, in the middle of the fire, I had convinced a major magazine that a story on Devil's Hole would be rather good. The magazine had given us a go-ahead, depending upon the pictures we could get. The National Park Service, however, didn't want unnecessary people stepping on the pupfish and that was that. The park service had given me permission to make one dive, as a safety diver for the scientist who counted the fish every month. I had convinced Jack to go with me to Death Valley to see what photos we could scare up. There were other springs and sinkholes that could be part of the story. Now we couldn't find the springs and sinkholes, nor Devil's Hole itself.

Jack McKenney is an old friend of mine with whom I'd worked on other underwater assignments. I wondered what he was thinking now as he looked at the wild dogs and buckshot salutation.

"What the heck," said Jack. "Let's give it a try."

I was relieved to hear that Jack's sense of adventure was far from dead.

We drove into the fenced area toward a tin shack set in the middle of a large collection of rusted bedsprings, old appliances, benches, kitchen sinks, machinery, and other odds and ends. The only thing missing from this permanent swap meet was a rusted-out car on its axles, a sight quite common in the desert.

Immediately, two big dogs charged at the car, barking and snarling, one at each door. "Nice doggy," said Jack. That was an enormous amount of optimism, the type Daniel must have had when he faced the lions that were supposed to eat him.

A man emerged from the tin house (without a gun). He didn't seem belligerent, and he called off the dogs.

"We're lost," Jack called out. "Could you tell us where Devil's Hole is?"

"Shore!" said the man. "Why don't you come in and sit a bit?"

This wasn't buckshot by any means. We proceeded to get out of our car, only to find that the wild dogs jumped up on us like big puppies.

"Down, boy!" yelled the man. He extended his hand to us. "Name's Rex," he said.

Jack and I introduced ourselves and told him what we were doing. "What do you know?" Rex said, "Follow me."

He led us over to an area of his yard which was fenced in by the circular ends of enormous wooden spools, and pointed off in the distance. "See that mountain over there?" he asked. "The very last one of that bunch?"

We said that we did.

"See that dark spot? Near the base of it?"

We made out the dark spot.

"That's Devil's Hole."

He drew a map for us in the dirt and told us how to get there. "You know," he said, standing up, "there's a hole right here, next door to me. A big one. Used to be bottomless until one of them atomic bomb tests caved the thing in."

Jack and I looked at each other.

"It's deep, you can dive in it," he continued. "Sand is boiling up all the time."

"We'd like to see it." I said. "Could we?"

"Shore!" said Rex. He gave us directions on how to get there through his property. "Leave the gate down when you come back through," he said. "So that the horses can get back in."

We went immediately to look at Rex's spring. It was exactly

what we had been looking for. It was 30 feet deep and the sand was boiling up at the bottom as he had said it did, like bubbling lava. Contrary to Rex's imaginative tale, the pool hadn't really been caved in by a bomb blast. Instead, it was a perfect example of the geologic phenomenon of the desert sinkhole, where water dissolves the bottom of the pool as it pushes up from an underground water supply. Our photographs would show perfectly this vital link in the desert water system.

We were really happy right then and drove back to thank Rex. He was in his tin house when we arrived, wrestling with some frozen orange juice cans on top of his wood-burning stove. "Can't get enough darn cans together to organize this," he complained. He turned to a cupboard over a crude wooden table and fished around for what I thought would be something to organize the orange juice. Instead he pulled out a cereal bowl, filled it with cat food and set it on the floor. A gray kitten materialized out of nowhere and began to eat. Rex went back to his orange juice project. Watching over him from the wall was Christ, who looked out over the one-room desert cabin in a handsomely framed print of *The Last Supper*.

I asked Rex his last name.

"Just start spelling," he answered. I got out my pen.

"S-c-h-n-e-e-h-a-g-e-n," he spelled.

"Schneehagen?" I asked. "What nationality is that?"

"American," said Rex.

Jack and I were in the highest of spirits as we drove toward our lodgings in Furnace Creek. We now knew where Devil's Hole was and Rex Schneehagen was a gold mine. The next day we'd be able to dive and photograph in Rex's spring. We'd get the magazine assignment for sure. It was all a stroke of luck.

Then it hit us. Adventure was really the thin line between
boom or bust. We'd both felt completely helpless five minutes
before we'd met Rex Schneehagen, and now we felt grand. We
realized, too, that if everything had been set up for us without the
risk of failure, we would have had the security of knowing exactly
what we were doing, but none of the thrill of chance. Chance is
the very stuff adventure is made of. We might have fallen flat on
our faces, but since it looked as if we might make it, the sense of
victory seemed ever so much sweeter. We'd done it on our own,
made our own discovery, broken our own trail. Though others
had probably done it a thousand times before, it made no
difference; we had done it all ourselves.

I had heard about Devil's Hole just after I had returned from
exploring the freshwater caves of South Australia. I was sitting
around the living room of my friends Chris and Hadda Swann
one evening, telling them about the caves. I told them about
diving in the middle of a sheep pasture, underneath a forest and
a road, and about what if felt like to crawl and swim around
darkened, flooded passageways and rooms with light and lines.
Chris, who is British, jumped up with an "Aye saye," and ran to
get something from another room. He came back with an old
film festival program describing Merl Dobry's documentary on
Devil's Hole. In the program was a diagram of Devil's Hole,
showing what was underground and underwater, describing
what the hole was about and how it had been formed. I had heard
of Devil's Hole because of the pupfish issue, which had been U.S.
news, but I had never imagined that it would be so big, deep, and
complicated. From the diagram I could see there were multitu-
dinous passageways that angled off the main shaft. A narrow slot
edged to one side of the main shaft and opened into a giant air-

filled room underneath the mountain. Below a narrow passageway that descended to 160 feet was an enormous chamber of water that continued to at least 260 feet. No one had bottomed the hole, so its exact depth was unknown.

From the diagram and description, Devil's Hole appeared to be more exciting than any of the holes we'd dived in Australia. In looking at all of this material, I found myself becoming a little excited and curious.

The desert of Death Valley is geology in action, a silent, eternal kiln where panoramic rocks are fired day after day in sun that never quits. It is a harsh, untamed land that bears names like Furnace Creek, Desolate Canyon, Badwater, Dante's View, Hell's Gate, and Ash Meadows—home of Devil's Hole. The land seems fluid still, with its boiling, bubbling, moving, cracking and faulting earth now frozen in time. Mountains have spilled their volcanic ooze down bumpy canyons in rollercoaster paths of heated chocolate bordered by vanilla-colored pumice and sand. Dark rivers of black ash snake through mounds of caked mustard clay. Sharp, jagged crags, once buried deep in granite, shoot upward in violent explosions that are frozen in midair. The land is untouched by man because it is so untouchable. The only evidences of his being there are the occasional giant anthills where he has dug for minerals. Zeolite, the soft green, moonlike rock used to filter water, is piled up beside the roads. Old scars in the sides of mountains reveal abandoned gold or silver mines. But it is borax, the "white gold" of the desert, that is important here. Borax gave Death Valley its 20 mule-team history.

It was hard to imagine that at one time the dry, salt-encrusted desert on which we stood was a fertile, green, freshwater land of lakes and rivers. It was even harder to imagine that such an enormous amount of fresh, pure water was now underground, hidden from sight.

Sand dunes in Death Valley. Photo by Jack McKenney.

The geologic history of Death Valley tells us how this water system came to be. In late Precambrian and Early Cambrian time, Death Valley was beneath the sea, as much of the world was. The shoreline, it is estimated, lay to the east, near modern Las Vegas. By the Middle Cambrian to Permian time (550 million years ago), the skeletal carcasses of innumerable generations of corals, shellfish, and other sea animals had created an enormous mass of lime and sand. This mass then consolidated into a limestone and dolomite layer more than two miles thick in some areas, perhaps only tens of feet in others.

In Mesozoic time (225-65 million years ago), a chain of volcanoes arose along the present Sierra Nevadas, and the sea withdrew. The limestoned Death Valley region became a highland.

Limestone is porous, and the rainfall from a big area of Nevada, northeast of Ash Meadows and Death Valley, collected underground, forming a major water table. As it ran in the direction of Ash Meadows, this water dissolved the limestone. In some areas where it collected and pooled, it ate upward through the limestone until the surface land collapsed downward, creating the sinkhole. This was the same geologic process that had created the sinkholes in South Australia.

Devil's Hole, on the other hand, is a flooded earthquake fault, formed by one of the earthquake or faulting actions of the Mesozoic period. Extending into the earth from the base of an unnamed mountain in the Amargosa Desert, it filled with the water that permeated the rest of the underground area. In Devil's Hole, the water began to eat away at the limestone fissures, enlarging the caverns and creating new passageways, new tunnels, and chambers.

The bottom of Rex Schneehagen's spring in Ash Meadows, officially called Big Spring, was disintegrating before our eyes and, during some geologic time down the road, the bottom of that spring would collapse, perhaps opening up into some enormous chamber such as that of Devil's Hole. Or, perhaps it would only be a shallow pool or underground river. One needs X-Ray eyes to see what is underneath that bubbling sand pile.

At 8:00AM the next morning, Jack and I arrived at Devil's Hole.

It looked like a prison camp sunk into one side of a volcanic mountain. Giant coils of barbed wire tangled with the metal mesh of a high, impenetrable fence to seal off the confining pit from the outside world. At one end was a heavy gate, sealed shut with a massive chain and padlock. Just inside the gate was a steep rock cliff, bridged by a wooden ladder propped against its uppermost ledge. A rock slope descended the rest of the way to the bottom of the cavern, where a rectangular trough of water emerged from underneath the mountain. That trough of water was bottomless, a flooded earthquake fault.

At 8:30 Jim Deacon arrived. So did Pete Sanchez from the National Park Service, Bob Yoder from the U.S. Fish and Wildlife Service, and a representative from the Bureau of Land Management. It was all serious business. Pete Sanchez, who'd been with the Park Service in Death Valley for 12 years, sat with me on a rock and in casual conversation I asked him if he had ever found anything valuable while poking around in the desert sands.

"Sure!" he said.

"Like agates?" I asked.

"No!" he answered emphatically. "Nothing monetary. Only plants and animals. Things other people might not think valuable, things you can't put a price on. But to me those things are valuable."

Pete Sanchez was not only resource management specialist with the Park Service, he was head of the desert pupfish council. It was obvious to me he was the best possible choice for both jobs.

Jim Deacon prepared for the morning dive. He laid down a narrow bridge of boards over the shallow shelf of bright green algae where the pupfish live, and then we geared up. There would be three of us on the dive—Jim, me, and Park Service safety diver Bob Todd.

As I tight-roped across the narrow boards in my heavy diving gear, I looked down at the tiny fishes, each one of them no bigger than a minnow. They swam leisurely around their shelf, picking at algae, oblivious to the human *sturm und drang* above them. They didn't know about the badges or the barbed wire. Most likely they were oblivious to the fact that there are so few of their numbers left in the world. They are tiny little fishes under enormous lock and key.

I carefully put one foot on the very edge of the shelf and lowered myself backward into a drop-off of clear, blue water. As I waited for the others, I looked down through my facemask and could see the first ledge below me at 30 feet. Swimming in the 92°F water was like swimming in nothing. It was so clear that visibility might have been 300 feet. It was like soaring in air, the closest thing to flying I'd ever known.

As the three of us sank through that giant, water-filled crack in the earth—so deep it hadn't been bottomed—I was reminded of how I felt during our exploration of the Australian sinkholes. The feeling of anticipation, wonder, and excitement at swimming into a dark underground, underwater cave was just as strong now as it had been then.

The sides of the main shaft of Devil's Hole consist of white limestone, laid down 550 million years ago and chiseled over the years by water into smooth slopes on either side. Rust-colored organic material on top of the elevated ridges of stone created an ethereal, other-worldly effect. At 60 feet, I turned and looked up toward the surface. The bright blue of the shallow water at the surface illuminated the main shaft and silhouetted the sloping wall on the right side. From where I hovered, I could see people standing around on the rocks above, almost as clearly as if there had been no water between us. Just as distinct was the long, rectangular lamp that hung over the water, positioned over the pupfish shelf and turned on when algae production needs a boost. Another shaft of light beamed down from behind a rock in back of the main entrance. The slope of limestone leading up to it created a narrow ledge against the ceiling of the cave.

I turned again toward the bottom and the three of us switched on our lights. We sank to 90 feet where an enormous flat stone called Anvil Rock signaled the deepest part of our dive. This stone, shaped like an enormous anvil and obviously shaken loose from above, marked the deepest spot where the pupfish wander from their shallow shelf. Jim started counting at this point while I beamed my underwater light down beyond Anvil Rock to see what I could see. I knew that below Anvil Rock was the narrow funnel that went to 160 feet and the deeper chamber. Merl Dobry had explored this chamber, the area that had invited trouble in the past. Nitrogen narcosis had robbed at least one diver of judgment and common sense here. It was in this chamber that the two divers had disappeared in earlier years, their bodies never recovered. One needed good lights and a safety line system to explore Devil's Hole.

The most exciting area of Devil's Hole that Merl had described was Brown's Room. This huge, air-filled, underground chamber is accessible only through a narrow slit that angled off to the left of Anvil Rock. Merl had talked about the squeeze in getting past the opening, about the enormous, cathedral-like room that opens into an air-filled chamber beneath the mountain.

While poking around Anvil Rock, I saw a line, tied permanently around a rock, angling up through the narrow passageway that leads to Brown's Room.

I looked at the other two. Jim was counting fish at about 60 feet and Bob was watching him count. I wasn't going to see Brown's Room on this dive, so I swam up and joined the others.

Later, over pizza at a mid-desert saloon near the California/ Nevada border, Jim explained that the pupfish had been stranded in Devil's Hole 20,000 years ago, when the freshwater system of the desert began to dry up and recede. Because Devil's Hole was one of the higher habitats, these creatures were the first to be stranded, the first of the desert pupfishes to evolve into its own, distinct species.

The continuing desiccation of the area resulted in similar isolation and consequent reduced survival odds for other popu-

Dr. Jim Deacon and Hillary Hauser at Devil's Hole sign, which is above the hole itself. Photo by Jack McKenney.

lations of desert pupfish. The Tecopa and Shoshone pupfish were already extinct, and the Warm Springs pupfish were endangered. Other desert pupfish in the area, such as those in Crystal Spring, were all right for the moment, said Deacon, because at that desert level, the water is still flowing between the springs and ponds where the fish live and propagate.

All pupfish species have tolerated periodic difficult living conditions, usually associated with summer heat. When the sun is hot, their habitats dry up. Some pupfish survive parched summers in homes the size of a teacup. When water evaporates in these limited living quarters, salinity levels increase. The desert pupfish, Jim said, is one of the few fish in the world that can tolerate such concentrations of salt. The fish also withstands freezing temperatures in winter and a host of other difficulties, which include competitive, foreign species of fish and crayfish that compete with the pupfish for food and space.

The irony is that the adaptable little fish probably cannot withstand what human beings want to do to it. Yet another battle was brewing in Ash Meadows over water rights at the very moment Jack and I were there. The pupfish was again threatened by a land development scheme that planned to turn 13,000 acres of Ash Meadows into a recreational/housing/golf course development. It was going to be a war for water, and again, the Devil's Hole pupfish were going to be under the gun.

While we sat in the mid-desert saloon, Jack played devil's advocate and put forth the loaded question to Jim. "Why save the pupfish?" he asked.

Jim Deacon is one of those rare individuals whose work is serious, but who doesn't take himself seriously. He answered the question as if he had answered it many times, yet he was just as interested in the concept of what he was saying as if he'd thought about it for the first time.

"Two ways of looking at that question," he said. "One, if you value the earth, then you must also value the way it functions. Extinction of a species is a momentous event, because it removes one irreplaceable role in the functioning of the earth. Man is causing extinctions at an alarming rate. If the process continues, the resulting instabilities will affect the way the world works, making it less reliable for humans, as well as for other populations of animals.

"The other thing," he continued, "is that every living species represents a complex living system—a library of information. If man's uniqueness is his ability to know, then we have to protect that library of knowledge, which in this case is a live pupfish."

Deacon sat back and thought.

"Actually, do you know what the best answer is?" he said. "It's because they're here. That's all the reason you need."

Jack and I later went to dive in Crystal Spring, fed by Devil's Hole more than two miles away. When I free-dived to the bottom of the spring, I felt the enormous rush of water coming in from

Just inside the gate that seals Devil's Hole off from the outside world, a wooden ladder leads the way to the water. Photo by Jack McKenney.

the bottom, almost 4,000 gallons per minute. At the height of the controversial pumping of the underground water supply of the desert, the water pressure in Crystal Spring had declined to 1,670 gallons per minute, less than half its normal capacity.

Crystal Spring is one of the bigger holes in the area. The smaller pools, under such abuse, would literally dry up, never to return, even if the pumping were stopped. Once dry, always dry— that's how it works. The main flow of water in Crystal Spring comes in at its deepest part, in 30 feet of water. As we swam around the other areas of the spring, we saw the water pushing in from beneath the limestone bed, creating little circles of bubbling sand where the pupfish liked to congregate. It was as if they enjoyed the massage they got from the miniature water jets, or perhaps there was an oxygenation of the water they took advantage of.

There is plenty of water in Crystal Spring. There also seems to be an infinite amount of it in Devil's Hole and in the entire network of the desert's underground passageways. However, what happens in one spot affects another almost immediately. The system is fragile, temperamental. The water is the arterial life blood which cannot be siphoned lest the veins collapse.

We dived a number of the desert sinkholes, but in my mind I could still see Brown's Room and the permanent safety line tied around the rock leading up to it.

Some weeks later, Jack and I returned to Devil's Hole.

We carefully laid down the narrow bridge of boards over the shallow shelf where the pupfish lived and we geared up quickly. We stepped on the very edge of the shelf and lowered ourselves backward into the flooded drop-off. With our powerful underwater lights switched on, we swam quickly to the first ledge below, at 30 feet. Even in the dark, the water was warm and clear. We sank down through the main shaft until we were at Anvil Rock, at 90 feet. Again, I saw the permanent safety line and pointed it out to Jack. We quickly went for the line.

With our lights picking the way through the narrow, dark crack, I followed Jack along the safety line, which I held in my left hand. The back of my tank scraped the limestone wall over head as I pulled myself along on my stomach through the narrow opening. When we cleared the opening, we were at the bottom

Hillary Hauser swims down to Anvil Rock in Devil's Hole. The 92°F water was crystal clear. Photo by Jack McKenney.

of the cavern I'd been told about. Our lights illuminated the entire, flooded room. Enormous limestone walls rose from 80 feet and conglomerates of granite jutted through the whiteness of the limestone to create a submerged work of art. The white line led upward through the dark cavern.

Following the line, we rose through the clear, transparent water. It was still as warm as at the entrance of the main shaft because this water is heated by the depths of earth rather than by sunlight.

The reflection of my light hit the surface of the water, becoming silver as mercury against the bright white walls.

Because of the clarity of the water, it was almost impossible to tell the depth in which we swam. We had moved from 90 feet to the surface in a matter of minutes.

When we broke through to air, I was completely stunned by what I saw. The cavern of Brown's Room is enormous, probably 50 feet from the surface of the water to the ceiling. About ten feet above us, a dry passageway led off into a dark crack, another passageway. According to the diagram of Devil's Hole, that dark crack turned down again into yet another water-filled chamber. The walls of the main chamber were rusty brown and ancient. We were completely sealed off from the outside world, underneath a mountain in a Nevada desert. It was like a scene from *The Phantom of the Opera*.

We pulled our regulators out of our mouths and took a taste of the air. It was musty and we didn't know the quality of it, so we immediately switched back to our regulators. I turned off my light, Jack turned off his. Instantly, the room became pitch black. That was enough. We turned our lights on again and headed down, free-falling along the safety line until we came to the narrow crack that led us back to the main shaft. We squeezed through the passage, inching our way along on our bellies like snakes, and we came out an Anvil Rock. Together, we rose through the main shaft until we were back at the first ledge at 30 feet. Here, we stopped to have a long, close look at the tiny fishes.

The Devil's Hole pupfishes are living in a palace fit for the king of the fishes—the Eighth Wonder of the World.

MARTY SNYDERMAN

An assignment photographer, cinematographer, author, and speaker, Marty Snyderman specializes in the marine environment. His real love is filming animals that are large or rarely filmed, such as dolphins and whales, and those creatures that are often perceived as dangerous, such as sharks. His articles and photographs have appeared in publications worldwide and his film work has been seen on most major networks. A teacher of underwater photography and marine sciences consultant for the San Diego Unified School District, Snyderman also leads specialized dive tours. He is the author of a book, *California Marine Life*, published by Marcor in 1988.

MARTY SNYDERMAN

Diving the Outer Edge
of Adventure

am having a hard time concentrating today. There is, ever present in my mind, something that makes me think about tomorrow. I try to avoid my thoughts. For a few brief moments I almost forget, but thoughts about tomorrow return, inching forward, capturing my attention. I ask myself, "Am I ready?" As always, I reassure myself that in the open ocean I'll be at my best, alert and relaxed. And I am certain I'll be totally, yes totally, involved.

My equipment is ready and all that remains is anticipation and the worrying about things I couldn't control, such as weather and water conditions. I wish I had something to do to keep me busy, but when I find something to do my mind wanders—I just can't concentrate on the present. I catch myself looking at the clock every few minutes, but I can tell by the feelings in my stomach what time it is. I find myself half-heartedly wishing that tomorrow would go away but what I really wish is that tomorrow were here.

The alarm goes off, rudely awakening me from the security of sleep. It is still dark outside but I am up in a second. Fully awake, I am in my car and on my way to Howard Hall's. From there we will go over to the garage, grab our gear, and head for the boat—on our way to open water. We will spend our day in water more than 4,000 feet deep, 30 miles out to sea, exploring the Pacific Ocean. In mid-water we will observe and photograph the incredible variety of life found off the San Diego coast. And too, I am absolutely certain I will be outside the protective confines of a shark cage within touching distance of more pelagic sharks than I can count. This fact, more than any other, dominates my thoughts.

Howard and I will meet Larry Cochrane, Steve Earley, Fred Fischer, and Rick Geisler at Rick's boat. I know the conversation will be light and funny. My best friends have a way of making the hard times, the tense times, into the funniest of times. I am sure someone will ask Howard if he still remembers us, his old friends, or if he has replaced us with beautiful people from the jet set owing to his recent success as a television cinematographer. I am sure Howard will carefully remember not to use any of our names as he points at Larry and asks me who he is. Larry is the guy who helps Howard design and build his camera systems and they must spend at least three hours a week together. Rick will tease Steve about not yet shaving. We'll kid Larry about spending his life as a fireman getting cats out of trees, Fred about any and everything as he is especially vulnerable, and as for me, I just don't hear what they say anymore. But always, despite the laughter, I am trying to come to grips with the realization that I very willingly got myself involved, that I can't get out of it now, and that I wish I were already there. For today we are not just dreaming our dreams or sharing our dreams, today we are living our dreams, exploring and photographing a part of this planet's environment that few people get to see.

Finally, 25 miles out to sea, Larry cuts the engine. I am much closer to the sharks than I was three hours ago but I can't see them. Rick and Fred put some fish scraps into a chum bucket, put the bucket into the water, and with a little wind we will have a good slick in less than an hour. We all place our bets as to when we will see the first shark. We sit and wait and stare at the water and think our private thoughts.

"Here's one, it's a blue shark," Fred's voice pierces the silence. We all jump up, look over the rail, and sure enough, just like he said, there is a blue shark swimming up the chum line directly toward the bait bucket. We have all seen that sight at least 50 times before but we watch, somewhat mesmerized, as the blue approaches and bites the bucket. The adjectives that so often describe sharks enter my thoughts. The words powerful, graceful, efficient, streamlined, and predator quickly come to mind. Their predatory capability is what strikes me at this moment. Stan Waterman calls them magnificent creatures of the sea, but right now it is just a very big shark.

I know the time is near. After a little more than an hour sharks begin to circle the boat and we decide to start getting ready. We put the shark cage into the water, prepare our gear, and get ready.

At this moment my guts hurt. I can't catch my breath. My mouth is dry. Nothing seems funny. I can hear Larry saying, "There are at least ten. Two are better than seven feet." I wish I were anywhere but here. And yes, I ask myself in all seriousness why I am doing this. Everyone is looser than I am, I think, although no one is saying much. Howard asks, "Are you ready, Marty?" I reply, "Let me wash my mask one more time." I don't see how I can get out of this now. Maybe I'll feel better once I am in the water—can't be worse.

Blue sharks are bold and curious. They show no fear of divers and come unnervingly close. Photo by Marty Snyderman.

I am approaching the swim step. Splash! Yesterday's tomorrow has just arrived. God get me out of these bubbles. I can't see a thing. Turn around and look. Look up. Thoughts are racing through my mind but my body can't keep up. I tell myself, "Relax a little, nothing has bitten you yet."

As I look around and try to come to grips with the situation, the scene seems somewhat unbelievable. These sharks are so graceful. They appear to be undisturbed and unaroused by our presence. Look at that expressionless face. Reminds me of Howard. I'll have to remember to tell him that. I realize I have regained my sense of humor.

Suddenly, just as I knew it would be, everything is fine. Magic, absolute magic. On the boat when I was completely safe, I was dying inside. Now, suspended in innerspace swimming next to some of Nature's least predictable and most formidable predators, I feel totally exhilarated. The feeling is not the thrill

Blue sharks are graceful, not especially fast animals, that seem undisturbed by the presence of divers. Photo by Marty Snyderman.

of being a macho man, although I understand others who might suspect that it is. The feeling is more closely related to the fact that I live in a society where so often, technology controls my life. Here everything is so simple. I feel in control today, a simple person trying to photograph a simple animal.

The blue sharks are, as usual, bold and curious. If we remain still they will swim close enough to touch, too still and they will bite. The blues are perfectly designed for their element and their function in life. Even though I have been in similar situations, working with pelagic sharks in the open ocean during the last four years, I feel lucky to have the chance to see it all today.

Some sharks have remoras. One has the imprint of another shark's jaw next to its dorsal fin. Another is missing part of a pectoral fin. I try not to let my imagination run wild and create a story about how that pectoral fin disappeared.

Larry and Howard are going to hand feed blue sharks today. Both are very experienced at it and while it takes some guts to do, it is not crazy if one has the 15 years of combined experience with sharks Larry and Howard have. They have studied and photographed many aspects of shark behavior. The blues aggressively eat the bait Howard offers. The blues begin to get a bit more worked-up, a little more aggressive, and I am anxious to photograph the action.

Two blue sharks bump me before I see them. I tell myself to pay attention but I know I am concentrating. I don't really feel a sense of danger for myself or for Larry and Howard. I know we could get hurt by blue sharks, but badly hurt, in the particular situation we are experiencing is highly unlikely. Howard and Larry pull their act off without a hitch, almost controlling the blues with the bait.

Today we are especially lucky. We have seen several salp chains floating through the water. They appear and disappear with the current. There is one purple striped jellyfish. Simple animals but beautiful to see. Owing to recent storms part of a kelp paddy floats by and baitfish hiding in the loose kelp swarm around us. I think the baitfish are beautiful but the sharks seem to be irritated.

I wonder if a sea lion will appear today. Once Larry and I saw a sea lion bite a mako shark four different times and chase it away from the shark cage where we were filming. I bet few people have seen a sea lion bite a shark. I only know of two. And on another recent mid-ocean dive Howard and I saw a marlin underwater. Though we were not close enough to photograph the fish, my mind recorded that memory for me.

We make one more dive, but the diving day ends much sooner than I want it to. Aboard the boat on the way back to San Diego we all feel pretty good.

I'll sit alone on the bow for a few minutes on the way in and

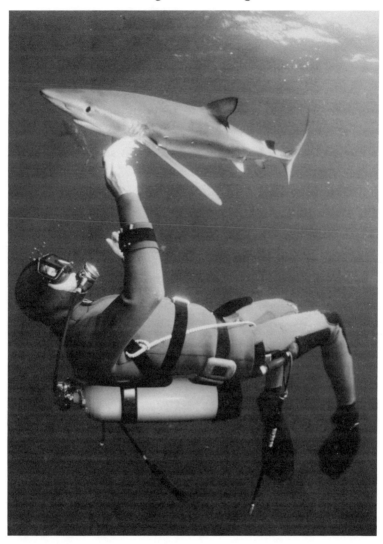

Howard Hall atempts to hand feed a small blue shark. Photo by Marty Snyderman.

think my private thoughts. I feel good inside. I tried hard to do well today and it is fun to be so totally involved in life. My friends are doers and goers. We push each other to new limits and higher heights. I see more in life and try a little harder to get that magic photograph just because these guys make me want to do so. I realize now that they were just as scared, as anxious, and as excited as I was, although they wouldn't say so.

Whale Chase

he job description sounded so simple. Howard Hall and I were to film gray whales in the beautiful waters of San Ignacio Lagoon, Baja California. We would be working for Franz Lazi, a noted West German filmmaker. I had pictured myself in those beautiful waters filming the most cooperative of whales. In my mind's eye the footage was exceptional. As the story unfolded in my head the certainty took root that this material would keep me on the film festival circuit for years to come.

In the lagoon, however, things just didn't go as planned. The first few days neither of us even had the opportunity to get in the water with whales. We simply baked, as opposed to basked, in the Baja sun. Then we suffered the frustration of whales that came close enough to get us into the water but not close enough to film.

Another encounter went something like this. We were approached by a "friendly" gray whale that swam without hesitation toward our boat. There was a collision that sent cameras and bodies flying like leaves in a storm. The 80,000 pound animal apparently liked the contact—it backed up to bump us again and again.

All this while Howard and I conversed. "Howard, now is your chance. Get in and I'll hand you your camera."

"Sorry, Marty, I can't find my mask. Why don't you film this one?"

At this point we were interrupted by the whale, which knocked our outboard into the inflatable. We decided to pray. We replaced the motor and tried to film the animal by holding the camera over the side, but the whale suddenly departed. On the way back to the mother ship we tried to make our knees stop shaking as we discussed interesting topics such as alternative careers and the legalities of breaking contracts.

A little frustrated and a lot wiser about our task we continued on. The next day I again found myself bobbing on the surface, awaiting an approaching pair of whales. This time it was a cow and her calf. The baby was nearly 15 feet long and weighed more than two tons. The cinematographer in me wanted to swim toward the whales but the rest of me wasn't so sure. Previous mistakes had taught us that approaching the whales was not the thing to do. In the difficult diving conditions of the lagoon, it was best to let the mammals come to us. The twosome was only 50 yards away when it dropped below the choppy surface, the calf rolling down the mother's back as they submerged. The whales seemed to be heading right for me, but I had thought that before. Then I heard Howard excitedly directing me from the boat. "Look to your right, Marty, to your right!" With camera running, I turned and there before me was the face of a gray whale. I had just realized it was the calf when into view came the head of the cow. Unbelievable! For years I had wanted a good opportunity to film one gray whale and now there were two. In an instant, all of our previous efforts and frustrations became worthwhile. Although I felt no sense of impending danger, I was immediately overwhelmed by their size. The calf appeared small next to its mother, but it was enormous next to me. The mother's pectoral flipper looked to be as long as I am tall and with 15 foot visibility I could only see about one-third of the adult. I can never remember feeling so small.

For most of the next 30 minutes I was able to swim with and film these whales. It was one-half hour of pure diving pleasure. Initially the calf appeared to be more curious, or at least less cautious, than the cow. It boldly approached me, on several occasions coming to within inches of my camera. After a few minutes the cow seemed to become more relaxed as she, too, came closer and closer.

I was free diving in an effort to be as quick as possible, and in the restricted visibility both whales repeatedly faded out of sight. I must admit my knees became rather weak when they were beneath me. The thought of getting "a lift" from a rising gray whale sent crazy thoughts careening around in my head. Once the cow exhaled from directly below me and the stream of bubbles knocked me for a loop. That's right, the whale sent me head over heels just by breathing on me. I heard Howard laughing at me from the safety of the boat but somehow I just didn't see the humor.

Fortunately, neither animal surfaced from directly beneath me, both seemed acutely aware of my exact location. Their movements were incredibly precise and their body control excellent. I vividly recall watching them gently touching each other. They rolled against one another, rubbing their faces together. Then they would spin completely around for several revolutions. Using their pectoral flippers to control the spins and their powerful flukes to push themselves forward through the water, both animals maneuvered with remarkable ease. The surrounding water remained relatively undisturbed despite the presence of two playful whales. Calm, that is, until the cow decided to use her flukes to swim forward in a sudden burst of speed. The backwash alone from the ten foot wide flukes was enough to dislodge my mask. Bubbles went swirling toward the bottom as far as I could see and in an instant she was gone. The mother reappeared in a few moments to repeat the procedure. Several times she brought her flukes within inches of my head, but she never touched me.

I, however, could not resist the temptation and did reach out to touch my new-found diving companions. Their skin was rubbery to the touch and though I cannot be certain, I had the distinct impression that they were quite sensitive to the contact of my fingers. The mother had patches of barnacles and whale lice all over her body but the skin of the calf was relatively free of these pests. It is the combination of the white barnacle patches and the natural black skin that gives these whales their overall mottled gray color and, hence, their name.

As time passed I became more and more confident. I was able to swim right up to the baseball-sized eye of the calf for a tight shot but had to pay the price of having the calf return the favor. It proceeded to bounce me on its nose four times. I laugh about it now but in the water I wasn't quite sure how much of that I wanted to do.

When I ran out of film I asked Howard to hand me his camera. With a smile that said, "Don't hold your breath pal," he slid over the side of the inflatable into the water. Thinking fair is fair, I exited to help give him directions from the boat. In the water it was rather easy to lose sight of the whales due to prevailing water conditions. A buddy giving directions from the boat was like adding 50 feet to the visibility, so we worked with one of us in the water and one in the boat. As Howard ran low on film, the whales, for no apparent reason, decided to leave and that was the end of a most memorable diving experience.

A female gray whale lifts her head above the water to look at a boat load of photographers. Grays are covered with barnacles. Photo by Marty Snyderman.

None of the diving or filming would have been possible without the Mexican government, which granted us a special documentary permit to dive and film in the lagoon sanctuaries. And none of it would have been possible without some exceptional luck in weather and water conditions. Visibility in the lagoon is often well under ten feet, tidal currents up to eight knots are the rule rather than the exception, and winds often gust to 50 knots.

We were lucky, too, in that the whales chose this day to be so cooperative. In previous encounters we have not always been so fortunate. Once, Howard and I made the mistake of diving directly in front of a gray whale. I never saw the animal underwater as visibility was less than ten feet, but Howard did. By his account, "The whale looked startled, then tense, and it bolted away. I knew I was in trouble before I saw the fluke coming at me." The flukes smashed Howard's left arm and broke two ribs.

Witnesses on the boat said the whale seemed to throw its fluke at Howard in an exaggerated motion as if it were trying to hit him, and experts say whales throw their flukes at predators to ward them off. And, last year a whale pushed an inflatable on top of Howard's head, breaking his mask, but luckily he was not hurt.

Looking back on all those experiences I have had with gray whales, I realize that those dives were some of the best of my diving and photographic career. It is demanding and, in some ways, dangerous work, but the rewards are well worth the price that must be paid. The real treasure is the magic moments shared in the wilderness of Baja with a creature as magnificent as the gray whale.

CARL ROESSLER

There is probably no other diver in the world as well traveled as Carl Roessler. President of See and Sea Travel, the world's first and largest travel agency catering exclusively to divers, it is his job to seek out new areas and new experiences for clients. He does so with unwavering enthusiasm and incredible energy. An underwater photographer since 1967, his specialty is fish portraits and in that field he has few peers. Carl has written eight books, all of which are illustrated with his photographs: *The Underwater Wilderness, The Undersea Predators, Mastering Underwater Photography, Diver's Guide to the Cayman Islands, Coral Kingdoms, Diver's Guide to Australia, Under Tropic Seas* and *Great Reefs of the World.*

Kiss Your Regulator Goodbye

t was one of those triumphal days we have when a dive vacation is a total success. From a blue-vaulted sky the sun showered diamonds of light; in the water it seemed you could see forever.

This was Australia, the last day of a cruise in the Coral Sea. The entire week had been sublime. Our boat and crew were excellent, the weather benign. Our travels had taken us nearly 200 miles out to sea north of Cairns, to the fabled oceanic reefs for which Australia is justly famous.

Thinking back, we had been thrilled by one dive site with six, count em, *six* deadly stonefish, each the size of a football; there had been the delicately beautiful sailfin leaffish; the saucy mantis shrimp running all over the reef as if determined to observe and understand our noisy intrusion; and then there were the shark feeds, four of them in seven days, because the adrenaline started to flow and the divers wanted *more sharks*. Like all divers, their ignorance of the sea's gray sentinels had led them to fear; when they actually saw the sharks' behavior that fear gave way to addicted fascination.

Now, on our last full day, all that was behind us. Spirits were sky-high, for we were about to anchor at the famed Cod Hole on the outer Great Barrier Reef. This dive site is a place where, for many years, boats anchored behind the sheltering reef to clean their catches. Decades of having fish parts tossed into the water led to a Gathering of big groupers and other fish not above a free handout.

When divers began to go into the water here, they were delighted to find up to 20 massive grouper (known in Australia as potato cod), several Napoleon wrasse, green moray eels, grunts, small groupers and even reef fish in a *de facto* zoo. The closest parallel familiar to American divers would be Stingray City off Grand Cayman, though I believe the greater size and variety of creatures at the Cod Hole create a far more powerful experience.

I know it sounds disgusting, but what I do at the Cod Hole is stuff lots of cutup fish chunks inside the front of my wetsuit. When I'm in the water I can then pull out a chunk to offer the animals. Many times over the years I have fed these creatures and I felt I knew them and their routine very well. I remember a feed two years ago when one six foot green moray was inside my BC and another was coiled on my head like a turban.

What I failed to consider in my all too human way was that although I understood the nature of this feeding game, the fish hadn't figured it out.

In any event, I landed on the bottom, like some smelly Doctor Dolittle, and began dispensing fish chunks. In no time, 20 potato cod in the 60 to 100 pound class were all over me. These cod fearlessly lay their huge chins on your shoulder to let you know they want food. Soon the cod were joined by two of the big green morays swimming fully in the open and trying to stick their noses into my wetsuit. Around all this milled a swarm of red

This 300 pound Napoleon wrasse has figured out a way to get some of the fish chunks being fed big groupers at Australia's famed Cod Hole: He hovers above the feeding frenzy, darting in when least expected to snatch the food. Photo by Carl Roessler.

snappers and fusiliers. The result was a maelstrom of animals around me, so it is understandable that I missed registering a 300 pound Napoleon wrasse swimming in the open water above me.

What I did not know was that this behemoth had figured out his own version of this game. He would hover above the milling cod, humans, eels and other riff-raff; when he saw his opening he would appear as if out of nowhere to snatch the food.

Remembering that the food was inside my wetsuit under my chin, what happened next is understandable. One moment I was surrounded by cod and eels and reaching absent-mindedly into the suit for more fish and the next moment my regulator was yanked from my mouth and disappeared.

The huge Napoleon wrasse had merely miscalculated by a

couple of inches but the result was a stunned moment when I reached around and couldn't find the regulator. Oh, yes, and I was 50 feet down.

I have long advocated that everyone learn buoyant ascent techniques, on the theory that you can swim out of any mechanical failure by using them. Instinctively, I popped some air into my vest and levitated to the surface.

Floating there, feeling like an idiot, I laughed my head off, then glared down at the big wrasse. The regulator was scarred and the exhaust twisted, but had not been ripped from the tank as I thought in the first startled moment. The wrasse's assault had merely left the mouthpiece and hose tangled somewhere behind me where I couldn't reach it.

In retrospect, my sassy friend the wrasse reminded me of two things: first, humans are not the only smart creatures in the sea and we frequently get our comeuppance from crafty creatures we have underestimated; second, if you learn buoyant ascents and can use them instinctively, no equipment failure need be a problem.

Thanks a lot Mr. Wrasse but next time take it a bit easier on my teeth, OK?

CARL ROESSLER

Trapped Underwater
by a Great White Shark

The old cliche goes, "There are old pilots and there are bold pilots but there are no old, bold pilots." Like many cliches, it achieved that status for its utter, revelatory truth. Those of us who spend our professional lives in the water with animals eventually learn how close we can get to them without being nipped. It is now possible to photograph moray eels, sharks and other formidably armed marine animals in complete safety—well, almost complete!

The problem with experience is that the quest for more spectacular photographs lures us to shave our margins of safety thinner and thinner. Like the *torero* with the bull, we let the horns pass ever closer.

Every year since 1975 I have escorted a great white shark expedition to South Australia. Clients who have shared this adventure are members of the most exclusive club in diving—only six members per group and always the risk that our baiting may fail to lure any sharks. Sometimes we wait a day, two days, three days for the scent of our bait to reach out over the depths.

Over the years we have seen it all. Sometimes single sharks, sometimes two, once we had six. I have spent some 300 hours in the cages working to photograph these awesome and magnificent animals. I have sunk the cages and had the sharks swim over me; I have leaned out the cage door and held my camera into the face of a 16 foot beauty. I had achieved a beatific confidence that Big Fluffy would never really want to bite me. I was his chronicler, his Boswell.

Sharks are not vicious or vindictive animals. Forget *Jaws* with its off the wall *Moby Dick* theme. In truth, great white sharks are large, cautious predators lured by chum to approach our cameras. On numerous occasions we have hung bait near the cage and I have waited in the doorway, poised. As the great shark would approach the bait, I would lean out toward it, camera extended. I was astonished to see the shark veer off. So much for the mindless monster myth: These animals are very aware, very deliberate and definitely risk-averse. That's how they get to be so large.

This year, on the seventh day of our expedition, we had perfect conditions: clear water, calm seas, blue sunlit sky and four large sharks feeding. Armed with my mental aura of animal invincibility, I was leaning out the open door to get that perfect portrait of the huge shark that had just bumped our cage. I squeezed off three shots, then began to pull myself back inside. Halfway through the maneuver a second shark crashed into the cage right behind me, the frame hit my right elbow and I watched my Nikonos come out of my numbed hand.

The next few moments I can replay in slow motion. The camera, hanging momentarily in open water, the searing thought that I had 34 hard won pictures in it, the nightmare vision of a shark taking it in one bite if it fell. I lunged out of the cage and managed to bob it upward with my fingertips. I leaned farther and bounced it again–missed. I had no thought of the sharks or

While filming great white sharks from a cage tethered to a boat in South Australian waters, Carl Roessler dropped his camera. Getting it back was quite an adventure. Photo by Carl Roessler.

that I was now completely out of the cage. The camera slowly fell past my fingers; I knew if I lunged again I would fall free of the cage and I did, then, think about the sharks around me.

Reluctantly, I watched the Nikonos fall to the bottom at 35 feet—inert, exposed. It might as well have been on the moon. A shark could have taken it at any moment. I can now tell you authoritatively that a Nikonos lying on an empty bottom surrounded by huge sharks looks very lonely and forlorn!

It was time for fast action. I asked my cage partner to get back on the boat. I knew that by opening the petcocks on the flotation pontoons the cage would sink to the bottom, yet still be attached to the boat's hoist by a one inch thick rope. The elevator to hell was ready.

The cage went down so quickly I could hardly equalize. It crashed to the sand several feet from the camera and fell over on its side. It was definitely not the most graceful or controlled descent in history. Still, it got me to the bottom somewhere near the lonely Nikonos.

I looked at the camera, then at the immense sharks that

sailed by just above me. There was no time to waste, I only had half a tank of air left and lots to do. The tipped-over cage helped me with one problem: I could put my feet on the sandy seafloor through the viewing windows, lift the cage on my shoulders and walk it over to the camera. When I had lurched the heavy cage over to within inches of the camera, I opened the door, reached out and pulled the precious camera in. So far, so good.

Now it was time to get the heck out of there and get that cage back to the surface. The procedure was simple. As I closed the petcocks on the tipped-over pontoons, I looked at the sharks swooping within inches of me, evidently curious. What was the bait-in-the-box doing?

Pulling the first stage of my regulator out of my mouth, I stuck the mouth piece up to the hole to let a burst of air into the pontoon. Uh-oh. The mouthpiece didn't fit into the hole: The tipped-over inlet hole was *next* to the regulator, not above it, and the air fluttered away. I was stuck. There was a moment, just a moment, when my imagination asked me whether I finally had gone too far.

Just as I realized I could laboriously blow puffs into the pontoon with my snorkel, I looked up. One of my clients was filming me from the other cage which was still floating at the surface. Realizing my predicament he signaled the boat and the crew hauled me up.

Was I in danger? Not really. But I realize now that over the years I had fallen into a smug, Olympian mindset: "I *know* these sharks. It can't happen to me."

It can happen to anyone and it happens precisely because experience and knowledge and ambition cause you to shave the margin–until one day there isn't any.

SOURCES

Grateful acknowledgment is made for permission to reprint the following:

"I Think that I Shall Never See a Tank Boot Square Enough for Me," by Dick Anderson, appeared in *Skin Diver Magazine*, September 1988 and is reprinted here with permission of the author.

"One of the Best Trades I've Ever Made," by Dick Anderson, appeared in *Skin Diver Magazine*, May 1987 and is reprinted here with permission of the author.

"Abalone Divers Get My Goat," by Dick Anderson, appeared in *Skin Diver Magazine*, February 1983 and is reprinted here with permission of the author.

"Do You Dive a Lot?" by Dick Anderson, appeared in *Skin Diver Magazine,* January 1989 and is reprinted here with permission of the author.

"Halfway to Hell" by E.R. Cross, originally appeared in *Water World*, September/October 1957 and is reprinted here with permission of the author.

"Deep Rescue," by E.R. Cross, originally appeared in *Skin Diver Magazine*, December 1982 and is reprinted here with permission of the author.

"Salvage of the Squalus," by E.R. Cross, originally appeared in *Skin Diver Magazine*, October 1986 and is reprinted here with permission of the author.

"A Bigger Fish Story," by Richard Ellis, originally appeared in *Sport Diver*, January/February 1981 and is reprinted here with permission of the author.

"How to Paint a Whale," by Richard Ellis, originally appeared in *Catasus*, Volume 1, Number 1, 1986 and is reprinted here with permission of the author.

"Descent to the Monitor", by Rod Farb, copyright 1992 by Rod Farb.

"Mola Mola Encounter," by Stephen Frink, originally appeared in *Ocean Realm*, Fall 1989 and is reprinted here with permission of the author.

"Wetsuit Squeeze," by Katherine Green, originally appeared in *Skin Diver Magazine*, September 1989 and is reprinted here with permission of the author.

"Hammerheads by the Hundreds," by Howard Hall, appeared in *Skin Diver Magazine*, May 1981 and is reprinted here with permission of the author.

"Fantasy Flight," by Howard Hall, appeared in *Skin Diver Magazine*, August 1981 and is reprinted here with permission of the author.

"Night of the Squid," by Howard Hall, appeared in *Skin Diver Magazine*, August 1983 and is reprinted here with permission of the author.

"Playing Tag with Wild Dolphins," by Howard Hall, appeared in *Skin Diver Magazine*, July 1986 and is reprinted here with permission of the author.

"Mugged by a Squid", by Howard Hall, originally appeared in *Ocean Realm*, Spring 1991 and is reprinted here with permission of the author.

"Things I Wished They'd Told Me Before I Bought My Boat," by Eric Hanauer, was originally published as "A Diver's First Boat," in *Scubapro Diving and Snorkeling*, Summer 1986. It is reprinted here with permission of the author.

"Gold in Them Thar Hills," by Hillary Hauser, from *Call to Adventure*, copyright 1987 by Bookmakers Guild, copyright 1990 by Hillary Hauser. Reprinted with permission of the author.

"Devil's Hole," by Hillary Hauser, from *Call to Adventure*, copyright 1987 by Bookmakers Guild, copyright 1990 by Hillary Hauser. Reprinted with permission of the author.

"Beneath the Sulu Sea," by Jack McKenney, copyright 1992 by Jack McKenney Productions.

"The Bay of Dolphins," by Jack McKenney, copyright 1992 by Jack McKenney Productions.

"The Stingray Man," by Jack McKenney, copyright 1992 by Jack McKenney Productions.

"At Work with Cousteau," by Jack McKenney, copyright 1992 by Jack McKenney Productions.

"Shark Attack, A Love Story," by Christopher Newbert, originally appeared in *Ocean Realm*, Winter 1988 and is reprinted here with permission of the author.

"Kiss Your Regulator Goodbye," by Carl Roessler, originally appeared in *Skin Diver Magazine*, May 1991 and is reprinted here with permission of the author.

"Trapped Underwater by a Great White Shark," by Carl Roessler, originally appeared in *Skin Diver Magazine*, October 1990 and is reprinted here with permission of the author.

"Dive the Outer Edges of Adventure," by Marty Snyderman, appeared in *Skin Diver Magazine*, April 1980 and is reprinted here with permission of the author.

"Whale Chase," by Marty Snyderman, appeared in *Skin Diver Magazine*, January 1982 and is reprinted here with permission of the author.

"Whale of a Rescue," by Bob Talbot appeared as a Letter to the Editor in *Whalewatcher*, 1985. Copyright 1985 by Bob Talbot, reprinted with permission of the author.

"Dangerous Dudley Does Cayman," by Stan Waterman, appeared in *Skin Diver Magazine*, June 1984 and is reprinted here with permission of the author.